Yesterday, Today
and
Forever

Yesterday, Today and Forever

Jesus Christ and the Holy Trinity in the Teaching of the Seven Ecumenical Councils

Peter Toon

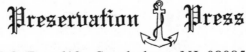

Preservation Press

P.O. Box 612 • Swedesboro, NJ 08085

For
**The Right Revd Keith L. Ackerman SSC, Bishop of Quincy
in the Episcopal Church of the USA,**

*who gratefully accepts the doctrinal decrees
of the Seven Ecumenical Councils as orthodox dogma
and
who has shown great kindness to the author's family.*

TABLE OF CONTENTS

Prologue

Christianity is one of the three major religions of the world which confess belief in and commitment to one God and one God alone (Monotheism); further, it is the one and only religion which is wholly based on Trinitarian Monotheism. Christians are those who have been baptized into "the Name of the Father and the Son and the Holy Spirit," and who receive in worship "the Blessing of God Almighty the Father, and the Son, and the Holy Spirit."

Christianity engages all aspects of the life of the baptized person, who is called to love God with all his heart and soul and mind and strength, and to love his neighbor as he loves himself. Christian worship is offered to the Father through Jesus Christ, the Son, and in the Holy Spirit, not only by the minds, but from the hearts and with the bodies of baptized believers.

The sacred Scriptures of the Old and New Testament, preserved by the Christian Church, are addressed not merely to the minds of hearers and readers, but to people as living, thinking, feeling and acting beings; the reading of the Bible, as well as the teaching and preaching from its pages, informs the mind, warms the heart and moves the will. There can be no true religion unless the affections of the heart are involved—e.g., desire, love, joy, fear (reverence) and peace. Yet the affections have to be guided by the mind (thus the expression "the mind in the heart") towards the right ends—i.e., enjoying and glorifying God forever. Further, the human will also has to be energized by the affections and guided by the informed mind so that the Christian obeys the Lord's commandments in word and deed.

We need to be clear on one important matter. The major statements and pronouncements of the doctrinal decrees of the Seven Ecumenical Councils are not addressed, as are the Gospels, in common-sense language and narrative form to the whole person to move him at all levels of his being towards God and his kingdom. No. They are addressed primarily to the mind in order to be understood, considered and received as truth. They declare what is right Christian teaching concerning (a) the relation of Jesus Christ and the Holy Spirit to God (i.e., to the One who is called "Yahweh" [LORD] in the Old Testament and "the Father" in the New Testament), (b) the full identity of Jesus Christ, One Person made known in two natures, who is "the same yesterday, today and forever" (Heb.13:8), and (c) the nature and use of icons.

In addressing the mind and providing clarity concerning what is true and what is false, the declarations from these Councils presume that right thinking is intimately related to right worship, right speech, right action and right behavior. This said, their primary function is to declare what is true and right and thus also to make clear what is false and wrong. For only those who rightly believe can rightly pray and rightly obey. Devout feelings and moral decisions will flow from right doctrine lodged in the mind and heart.

I have heard people, who know a little about early Church history and who are very conscious of wanting to be *modern* and *relevant* Christians, make comments such as the following concerning the Councils. (i) Because of their intellectual nature, the pronouncements of Councils seem to be intended only for those whose religion is primarily of the head and who understand Greek philosophical terms. (ii) Because they have apparently no concern for the feelings (which have such an important place in contemporary forms of the Christian reli-

10

gion), the doctrinal decrees appear to have no immediate relevance for those whose religion is primarily "of the heart." (iii) Because they insist not only on proclaiming what is true but also on anathematizing those who teach heresy, the Councils lack charity and are out of touch with modern ecumenism and ecclesiastical dialogue. And (iv) because the Councils belong to a period when Church and State were closely integrated and when there were no individual rights and no genuine freedom of speech, they belong to a totally different world and culture and thus have little or no relevance today.

Of course, there is some truth in what these people have to say, but it is certainly not the whole truth. They are missing much by dismissing the Councils too easily and quickly. It is reasonably clear to me that, in order to appreciate what the Councils achieved and what their legacy to the modern Church genuinely is, Christians today, even if well motivated, have to make a big effort to seek to understand the reasons why Councils were called, the way they addressed the doctrinal questions and problems of their times, and what their members thought they were giving to and providing for the Church of their day and of the future. Further, we need to have an appreciation of what has been called the development of doctrine—the relation between the way doctrine is presented and taught in the New Testament and the way it is presented and taught by the Councils.

This book is intended as a positive contribution to the fuller appreciation of what is the legacy of the Councils for the one, holy, catholic and apostolic Church today. It is written as simply as possible, bearing in mind that the solid subject matter does not lend itself to over-simplification!

In particular, the book is addressed to a growing number—not a vast but a worthy company—of people in America, who have entered on what I often call the "liturgical trail," a search for wholeness in worship and spirituality in the major, deeply historical traditions of Christendom. The "Canterbury trail" into classical Anglicanism is not as popular as it used to be in the 1960s and 1970s, primarily because the modern American Episcopal Church does not often support or express that classical Anglican Way today; more popular now for those on the journey are the "Antioch [or the Constantinople] trail," the "Roman trail" and a general "symbiotic [syncretistic?] trail" (which embraces East and West).

In this absorbing search for sound liturgy and right appreciation of the sacramental, symbolic and aesthetic dimensions of worship and spirituality, travelers are led sooner or later to discover the patristic period when the Ecumenical Councils convened and the Fathers wrote. In part, this is because they recognize that they need to know how the first major pastors and teachers of the Church sought to read, use and interpret Scripture. In fact, all roads of the liturgical trail appear to lead in one direction—back to the Fathers of the first five to eight centuries, to their Councils, to their Creeds, to their Episcopate, to their Canon Law and to their Liturgies.

Those who search for authentic origins in the patristic period represent, I suspect, a good proportion of those who buy the modern reprint of the nineteenth century edition of the translations of selected writings of the "Pre-Nicene, Nicene and Post Nicene" Fathers. Here such worthies as Irenaeus, Tertullian, Origen, Athanasius, Basil, Augustine, Cyril, Leo and John of Damascus may be encountered; and included in this multi-volume edition is one volume dedicated to providing a translation of documents from the Seven Ecumenical Councils and other synods. It was also printed on its own as a separate volume—H.R. Percival, *The Seven Ecumenical Councils of the Undivided Church* (New York and London, 1900). We shall have cause to refer often to this volume, which though dated in its historical information is still most useful for its translation of the texts.

I have also written this book for those who are members of the older Churches (which are committed to the dogmatic state-

12

ments of the Seven Councils as their received doctrinal heritage and teaching) and who have not yet wholly explored, recognized or benefited from that precious heritage. An illustration may help make the point. Often we have within our personal libraries valuable books we have never read and which we ought to read. Likewise, it is often the case that there is in the Tradition of the Church a legacy of which we are hardly aware and ought to become aware. I hope this modest book will serve to make people in the historic Churches aware of that legacy in terms of the dogmatic pronouncements of the Seven Councils.

And now a few words about the actual contents of the book. The main emphasis is upon exposition of dogma and doctrine and the difference between orthodoxy and heresy. To the modern ear and mind the distinction between these may seem at times merely verbal or minimal—even far-fetched. If so, all the more reason why I urge my reader to work hard at appreciating why the differences were regarded as crucial in the early Church! Therefore, I provide the important primary texts from the Seven Councils in English translation from the Greek or the Latin. And, while I certainly provide a general, simple, historical introduction to each Council and narrate the more important events and circumstances surrounding it, the emphasis is not upon the historical context as such. For greater detail, I refer my reader to the various histories of the Early Church and the Councils. My purpose is to provide what I hope is a reliable and readable introduction to an appreciation and understanding of the doctrinal debates and decrees.

In two of the three Appendices, I deal with two modern questions. Is the Creed of the Eucharist to be in the "I believe" or "We believe" form? And, is the formula, "God: Father, Son and Holy Spirit", correct?

FOR FURTHER READING

A useful and readable history of the early Church is *The Rise of Christianity* (Philadelphia: Fortress Press, 1984) by W. H. C. Frend. The only recent book on the Councils for the general reader is by Leo Donald Davis, S.J., *The First Seven Ecumenical Councils (325-787): Their History and Theology* (Wilmington, DE: Michael Glazier, Inc., 1987). In this book are valuable bibliographies for the further study of each Council, but the doctrinal decrees and canons are generally summarized rather than printed in full. The most accessible translation of the documents of the Councils is that of Henry R. Percival, *The Seven Ecumenical Councils of the Undivided Church,* vol. 14 of the *Nicene and Post-Nicene Fathers, Second Series* (Peabody, MA: Hendrickson Publishers Inc., 1994), originally published in 1900.

For those who desire to have the Greek and Latin texts, along with modern (and sometimes politically correct!) translations of them done by a team of Jesuits, there is the most useful Norman F. Tanner, S.J., ed., *Decrees of the Ecumenical Councils*, vol. 1 (Washington, DC: Georgetown University Press, 1991). The Latin and Greek texts in this volume are taken from G. Alberigo, ed., *Conciliorum Oecumenicorum Decreta* (Bologna: 1973).

Also of great help for the first four Councils is T. H. Bindley, ed., *The Oecumenical Documents of the Faith,* 4th. ed. (London: Methuen and Co., 1950). [This was the text I used when doing my B.D. degree in London University.]

PART ONE:

SEVEN ECUMENICAL COUNCILS

Though we gladly give great honor to the Councils, especially those that are General, we judge that they ought to be placed far below the dignity of the canonical Scriptures; and we make a great distinction between the Councils themselves. For some of them, especially those four, the Council of Nicea, the first Council of Constantinople, and the Councils of Ephesus and Chalcedon, we embrace and receive with great reverence—and we bear the same judgment about many others held afterwards, in which we see and confess that the most holy Fathers gave weighty and holy decisions according to the Divine Scriptures, about our Jesus Christ our Lord and Savior, and the redemption of man obtained through him.

Reformatio Legum Ecclesiasticarum, Church of England, 1553.

CHAPTER ONE

Nicea I (325)
and
Constantinople I (381)

We need to distinguish between the modern use of "ecumenical" (= "oecumenical") as in the expression, "the Ecumenical Movement," and its traditional use as in the expression, "an Ecumenical Council." The Ecumenical Movement, closely tied to the World Council of Churches, is a movement for the unity of Christians throughout the world. Here "ecumenical" means "worldwide" or "universal."

The Greek words, *he oikoumene*, literally mean "the inhabited world" (i.e., the Roman Empire). Thus, a Council to be ecumenical has to be called by appropriate authority and has to be representative of the whole Roman Empire. Further, an Ecumenical Council is a Synod, the decrees of which have found acceptance by the Church at large. Only Seven Councils merit the full title of "Ecumenical" since they are the only Councils whose decrees were wholly accepted by the Eastern and the Western branches of the Church—that is, by the Church as represented by the Pope of Rome and the Patriarchs of Constantinople, Antioch, Jerusalem and Alexandria.

Since the year 787, when the last Ecumenical Council met, the Orthodox Church has refused to call any of its synods or councils "ecumenical." This is true even of the Council of Constantinople in 869-870, which the Roman Catholic Church has designated the Eighth Ecumenical Council since the late Middle Ages. In fact, in the West only Seven Councils were deemed Ecumenical as late as the pontificate of Pope Gregory VII (1073-1085). Today the Roman Catholic Church claims that there have been a further thirteen "General Councils" (from Lateran I in 1123 to Vatican II in 1962-1965) which are truly "Ecumenical."

THE FIRST COUNCIL OF NICEA (325)

Iznik in Turkey, now a predominantly Muslim country, was the place where the first Ecumenical Council met. The Emperor Constantine summoned the Bishops of the Christian Church in his empire to meet together with him at what was then Nicea, a city of Bithynia, in 325. In his Letter to them, he explained that he intended to be both a spectator and participator in what would be done. He also stated why he had chosen this city—the excellent temperature of the air, ready access for the Bishops from Italy and Europe, and near to his summer palace at Nicomedia.

For Americans, the separation of Church and State is a fundamental belief which they confess with enthusiasm. In contrast, after suffering repeated persecution at the hands of imperial Rome, the early Christians heartily welcomed the support and protection of Constantine, who was sole emperor from 324, and who was eventually baptized by Bishop Eusebius of Nicomedia in 337. While there had been regional church synods and councils for over a century, the calling of an Ecumenical Council was only possible because of the personal involvement of Constantine himself. Further, when it was over, Constantine caused its decrees to have the force of imperial law. The Church and State were henceforth closely linked and the Roman emperors were necessarily involved in the calling and organization of the rest of the Ecumenical Councils.

The reason why Constantine called the Bishops to meet at Nicea was simple. He wanted to see the Church united and not divided. At the center of the divisions were the name and teaching of Arius, a presbyter of the church in Alexandria. His teaching, which made use of many quotations from Scripture, differed from that of his Bishop, Alexander, and from the received tradition of doctrine concerning the deity of Jesus. Arius and his supporters maintained with enthusiasm and learning that Jesus Christ is the highest and the best of all God's creation, but still a created being. That is, though highly exalted, the Son who is the heavenly Logos is not of the same divinity as the Father.

The precise number of Bishops present on May 19, 325, to hear the Emperor's opening speech and take part in the work of the Council is not known. Later the Council was known as "The Synod of 318 Fathers." This number is probably a symbolic figure, based on the number of Abraham's servants (Gen. 14:14). The Patriarchs of Alexandria, Antioch, and Jerusalem were present, but the Pope was represented by Legates.

Two things are reasonably clear from our fragmentary accounts of this Council. First, the genuine Arians were a small and hopeless minority; secondly, the means proposed and adopted to outlaw and exclude Arianism was a startling measure. After intense debate a Creed, containing the word *homoousios* (consubstantial), was approved. It was probably intended to be understood at a layman's not a professional philosopher's level—that is, that Jesus Christ is really and truly divine and not in any way a creature. Theologians saw in it deeper meaning, and the reason why some were hesitant both in and after the Council to use it was that it suggested to them the idea of Godhead broken into fragments.

The Creed with four anti-Arian anathemas was promulgated and signed by all the bishops except two. Further, twenty canons were promulgated. Decisions were also reached on the Melitian schism in Egypt and the Paschal controversy. Thus a synodical Letter was sent to the church in Alexandria and the Antiochene custom of following the Jewish reckoning of the date of Easter was condemned.

The Creed of the Council was probably based on the Creed of the church in Jerusalem and adapted so as to reject the Arian doctrine of Christ.

We believe in one God, the Father almighty, Maker of all things visible and invisible;

And in one Lord Jesus Christ, the Son of God, begotten from the Father, only begotten, that is, from the substance of the Father, God from God, light from light, true God from true God, begotten not made, of one substance with the Father, through whom all things came into being, things in heaven and things on earth, who for us men and because of our salvation came down and became incarnate, becoming man, suffered and rose again on the third day, ascended to the heavens, and will come to judge the living and the dead;

And in the Holy Spirit.

But as for those who say, There was when he was not, and, Before being born he was not, and that he came into existence out of nothing, or who assert that the Son of God is of a different hypostasis or substance (ousia), or is created, or is subject to alteration or change—these the Catholic Church anathematizes.

Since the Bishops spoke together in synod they said, "We believe..." However, the baptismal creed on which the Creed of Nicea was based began, "I believe..." In other words, before the Nicene Creed, creeds were for catechumens. At Nicea and at later Councils creeds were also for Bishops in synod and so began, "We believe..." (See further Appendix I, "I believe/We believe")

The pronouncing of the anathema upon persons with heretical opinions is based upon Scriptural example in the Old Testament and apostolic precedent in the New Testament. In Greek,

20

anathema means "suspended" or "cut off" and is used in verbal form by St. Paul in Galatians 1:8-9, where he writes of those who preach and teach a false message: "Even if we, or an angel from heaven, should preach to you a gospel contrary to that which we preached to you, *let him be accursed.* As we have said before, so now I say again, If any one is preaching to you a gospel contrary to that which you received, *let him be accursed.*"

The Canons promulgated by the Council may be summarized as follows:

1. Concerning castration of the clergy, and whether or not they should be suspended.
2. Concerning the need for time between the baptism of a convert and his being ordained to the presbyterate.
3. Concerning which woman may live with a bishop or presbyter or deacon.
4. Of the number needed to appoint and ordain a Bishop.
5. Concerning the excommunicated in one diocese, who ought not to be received in another diocese.
6. Concerning the forms of primacy which belong to certain cities (and thus of their Bishops).
7. Concerning the Bishop of Jerusalem.
8. Concerning those who are called the Cathars (*katharos*=pure) and their reception into the Catholic Church.
9. Concerning those who have been ordained to the presbyterate without proper examination.
10. Concerning clergy who denied the faith during persecution.
11. Concerning laity who denied the faith during persecution.
12. Concerning those who have made a renunciation of the world and then returned to the world.
13. Concerning giving Holy Communion to the dying.
14. Concerning catechumens who lapse.

15. Concerning clergy who transfer from city to city.
16. Concerning clergy who do not stay in the diocese where they are ordained.
17. Concerning clergy who practice usury.
18. Deacons should not give Holy Communion to presbyters or be seated above them at the Eucharist.
19. Concerning the disciples of Paul of Samosata and how they are to be received in the Catholic Church.
20. Concerning standing and kneeling on Sundays and in the season of Pentecost.

A study of these Canons gives a good indication of the pressing disciplinary problems in the Church caused by persecution, of the existence of sects, and of the ease of travel within the Empire.

In Part Two of this book, we shall examine in detail the theology of the Nicene Creed and the heresy of Arianism condemned by the Council.

THE FIRST COUNCIL OF CONSTANTINOPLE (381)

The history of the Church from 325 to 381 involves the relation of the Emperors to the Church and their support either of a form of Arianism or (more rarely) of the Orthodoxy of the Nicene Creed and its primary defender, Athanasius, Bishop of Alexandria.

From a theological point of view, the debates in this period— concerning the relation of Jesus Christ to the Father, and of the Holy Spirit to the Father and to the Son, and what kind of Holy Trinity is God—were most useful for the purpose of clarifying the truth, even if they were mostly acrimonious! They served in the long term to clarify and develop the doctrine of Nicea that Jesus Christ is *homoousios* (not *homoios* or *homoiousios*) with the Father and that the Holy Trinity is of Three Persons and one Substance or "One *ousia* in three *hypostases*."

During the reign of the Emperor Constantine from 325 until his death in 337 there was a widespread reaction among many churchmen against the perceived doctrine and the vocabulary of the Nicene Creed. This was led by Eusebius, Bishop of Nicomedia, but they knew that the Emperor would allow no change in the Creed and so they were careful in what they did. However, they were able to get him to agree to the deposition and exile of the three leading supporters of the *homoousios*, Athanasius of Alexandria, Eustathius of Antioch and Marcellus of Ancyra.

From 337 to 350 the western Emperor, Constans, supported the Creed in the Latin West and protected the Bishops who stood by it. However, the eastern Emperor, Constantius, did not favor the Nicene Creed and sided with Eusebius and other critics. Therefore, when Constantius became the sole Emperor in 350 it seemed as though there was the triumph of Arianism in the Empire. New Creeds declared that the Son is only like (*homoios*) the Father. But the opponents of the Nicene Creed went too far in their enthusiasm for novelty and in their rejection of traditional faith. A general reaction set in and their cause lost ground. Those who have been termed "Semi-Arians" or "Moderates" began to move towards the traditional supporters of the *homoousios*. By 381, there was not too much difference between those who now spoke of Jesus Christ being of "like essence" (*homoiousios*) and those who insisted on the "identical essence" (*homoousios)* with the Father.

The Emperor Theodosius I, convened the Council in Constantinople at the imperial palace in May 381 in order to unite the Church on the basis of the faith of the Creed of Nicea. Some 150 orthodox and 36 heretical bishops from the East took part in the opening sessions, but the 36 heretics soon left. The 150 orthodox remained to produce some Canons and a long theological document expounding the doctrine of the Trinity called "The Tome," in which was contained the Creed approved by the Council. Regrettably, this Tome has not survived as a whole.

We know of its contents from a Letter sent out in 382 by a local synod in Constantinople and preserved in the Decrees of the Council of 381.

Although neither western Bishops nor Roman Legates were present, the Council of 381 was eventually accepted in the West and came to be regarded there as the Second Ecumenical Council.

The Creed of this Council, contained in "The Tome," was probably an enlargement, strictly speaking, not of the actual Nicene Creed of 325, but of a local Creed developed from the Nicene Creed and used in a church as a baptismal Creed between 325 and 381. It is possible that it was the Creed used for catechumens in Constantinople at that time by Gregory of Nazianzus. Whatever its precise origins, it came to be called "The Faith of the 150 Fathers."

Today we call this Creed either "the Nicene Creed" (which technically speaking is inaccurate but was a term which came into use in the Middle Ages) or "the Niceno-Constantinopolitan Creed" (which is a mouthful!). At later Councils, the Creed of Nicea (that of the 318) and the Creed of Constantinople (that of the 150) were clearly distinguished and each one fully accepted.

The Creed of the 150 in the "I believe" form became the Creed of Catechumens in the East and from the late fifth century the Creed recited in the Eucharist there. It is found in the Divine Liturgy of the Orthodox Churches as it is also found (with the addition of the *filioque*) in the Divine Liturgy of the Western Catholic (i.e., Roman) Church. (See further Appendix I, "I believe/We believe.")

The Creed adopted by the Bishops declares:

We believe in one God the Father almighty, Maker of heaven and earth, of all things visible and invisible;

And in one Lord Jesus Christ, the only begotten Son of God, begotten from the Father before all ages, light from light, true God from true God, begotten not made, of

one substance with the Father, through whom all things came into existence, who because of us men and because of our salvation came down from heaven, and was incarnate from the Holy Spirit and the Virgin Mary and became man, and was crucified for us under Pontius Pilate, and suffered and was buried, and rose again on the third day according to the Scriptures and ascended to heaven, and sits on the right hand of the Father, and will come again with glory to judge the living and the dead, of whose kingdom there will be no end;

And in the Holy Spirit, the Lord and Life-giver, who proceeds from the Father, who with the Father and the Son is together worshipped and together glorified, who spoke through the prophets; in one holy, catholic and apostolic church. We confess one baptism to the remission of sins; we look forward to a resurrection of the dead and life of the world to come. *Amen.*

The major difference between the Creed of Nicea and the Creed of Constantinople is the longer third part on the Holy Spirit. While the Holy Spirit is not specifically said to be *homoousios* with the Father, he is said to be worshipped and glorified together with the Father and the Son—which is to say much the same thing!

The Canons promulgated by the Council may be summarized as follows:

1. Concerning the continuing validity of the decrees of Nicea I.
2. Concerning the privileges due to certain cities and the need for proper order in dioceses.
3. Concerning the Bishop of Constantinople being honored after the Bishop of Rome.
4. Concerning the invalid ordination of Maximus.

5. Concerning the Tome of the Westerners about Paul of Antioch.
6. Concerning accusations against clergy and who may bring them.
7. Concerning the reception of former heretics who embrace orthodoxy.

Again, as with the Canons of Nicea, these provide a glimpse into some of the problems being faced by the Church, especially in the Eastern part of the Empire.

The third Canon is important for our study. It states: **Because it is new Rome, the Bishop of Constantinople is to enjoy the privileges of honor after the Bishop of Rome.** In 330, Constantine inaugurated Constantinople as his capital. It was on the site of the old Greek city of Byzantium. This meant that the status of the Bishop there, who had been subject to the nearby See of Heraclea, began to rise until at the Council of Chalcedon (451) he was given the status of Patriarch (to which old Rome objected!). The rise of the status of the Bishop of Constantinople in the fourth century was seen as a threat by the Patriarchs in Jerusalem, Antioch and Alexandria, and especially by the latter. Rivalry between Constantinople and Alexandria was a major factor in some of the controversies in the Church in the fifth century.

In Part Two of this book, we shall examine the theology of the Creed of the 150 Fathers and note the heresies faced and rejected by them.

Before we leave the description of the Council of Constantinople (381), it will be advantageous to print a summary of the lost Tome (Confession of Faith) produced by this Council. This is found in the Synodical Letter of the local Council of Constantinople which convened in 382.

> **For whether we endured persecutions or afflictions, or imperial threats or the cruelties of governors, or any other trial from the heretics, we withstood all for the sake of**

the gospel faith (creed) as authenticated by the 318 Fathers at Nicea in Bithynia. This faith should satisfy you and us, and all who do not pervert the word of truth—for it is the most ancient, it accords with the creed of our baptism and teaches us to believe in the name of the Father and of the Son and of the Holy Spirit—believing, that is to say, in one Godhead and power and substance of the Father and of the Son and of the Holy Spirit, of equal dignity and coeternal majesty, in three perfect Hypostases, that is three perfect Persons. Thus no place is found for the error of Sabellius in which the Hypostases are confused and their individualities taken away, nor does the blasphemy of the Eunomians and Arians and Pneumatomachi (="Fighters against the Spirit") prevail, in which the substance or nature of the Godhead is cut up and some kind of later nature, created and of a different substance, is added to the uncreated and consubstantial and coeternal Trinity. We also preserve unperverted the doctrine of the incarnation of the Lord, receiving the dispensation of the flesh as neither without soul nor without mind nor incomplete, but knowing that he existed as perfect God, the Word, before all ages, and became perfect man in the last days for our salvation.

We shall return to this summary in chapter six, when we shall be addressing the subject of the Holy Trinity.

However, here we may note that one word has changed its theological reference and meaning since the Council of Nicea in 325. In the anathemas of Nicea, the word *hypostasis* is used as a synonym for *ousia*. Literally, *hypo-stasis* is "that which stands under" and refers to the permanent being which underlies the appearance of things. *Ousia* has the more abstract but similar meaning of essence or being. Because of the work of the Cappadocian theologians (for whom see chapter six), the word *hypostasis* was used in theology to refer to the subsistence of being, not to being itself—thus they spoke of the *hypostases*, that is, the subsistences of the Father and of the Son and of the

Holy Spirit in the Holy Trinity. At the same time, the word *ousia* kept its general meaning of "essence" or "substance" or "being" and was used of the deity, common to all Three Persons, in such statements as "one *ousia* and three *hypostases*".

FOR FURTHER READING

For the general background to and proceedings of these two Councils see Leo Donald Davis, S.J., *The First Seven Ecumenical Councils*, chaps. 1-3, and Peter L'Huillier, *The Church of the Ancient Councils* (Crestwood, NY: St. Vladimir's Seminary Press, 1995). The texts in English are in Henry R. Percival, *The Seven Ecumenical Councils*, chaps. 1-3. For the Greek and Latin texts see Norman P. Tanner, S.J., *Decrees of the Ecumenical Councils*, vol.1., pp.1-36. The history and meaning of the Creeds of Nicea and Constantinople, from which the texts cited in this chapter are taken, are presented in J. N. D. Kelly, *Early Christian Creeds* (London: Longmans, 1970). For the origin of the title, "Oecumenical" (= "Ecumenical") see Henry Chadwick, "The Origin of the Title, *Oecumenical Council*," *Journal of Theological Studies* 23 (1972): 132-55. On the religious and ecclisiastical role of the Emperors see Charles N. Cochrane, *Christianity and Classical Culture* (New York: Oxford University Press, 1944).

CHAPTER TWO

Ephesus (431)
and
Chalcedon (451)

The first two Ecumenical Councils addressed and set forth the orthodox doctrine of the Trinity—that is theology proper, of God as God-is-in-Himself and thus of the relation within the Godhead of the Father and the Son, the Father and the Spirit, the Son and the Spirit. The next two Councils focused on the actual identity of Jesus Christ as the Incarnate Word, the Son of God with His human nature and flesh—i.e., the doctrine of the Person of Christ. To say that Jesus is truly God and also truly Man, as the Creeds of the 318 and the 150 had declared, is to raise the question as to whether he is two persons joined together in perfect harmony or one Person who has two natures. This and related questions cried out for answers.

THE COUNCIL OF EPHESUS (431)

To appreciate this Council we need to be especially familiar with the names of two famous Bishops, Nestorius of Constantinople and Cyril of Alexandria, and one theological term, *theotokos*, a title given to the Blessed Virgin Mary. Nestorius opposed the use of the word *theotokos* ("God-bearer") alone, unless it was balanced by *anthropotokos* ("man-bearer"), but he preferred *christotokos* ("Christ-bearer"). His opponents took him to be teaching that within Christ there are not only two different natures, but also two different persons and that Mary gave birth to the human person with the human nature. In contrast, Cyril insisted that there is one and one only Person, the Lord Jesus Christ. Thus the human mother of Jesus Christ is truly *theotokos*, for her Son is the Son of God with his human nature.

Nestorius was condemned as a heretic at a Council in Rome in August 430. Therefore, he asked the Emperor Theodosius II to call a council in the East to establish his orthodoxy. With the agreement of his co-emperor, Valentinian III, and Pope Celestine I, Theodosius II summoned the Bishops to meet at Ephesus at the Feast of Pentecost, June 431. Two weeks after the feast, yet before the arrival of the Roman Legates or the eastern Bishops led by the Patriarch John of Antioch, Cyril of Alexandria actually began the council. Nestorius, who was in the city, refused to attend, claiming that his accuser was to be his judge. In his absence, his teaching was examined and condemned by 197 bishops.

When John of Antioch arrived, he set up a rival council to that of Cyril. However, the Roman Legates, who arrived after John, joined Cyril and confirmed the condemnation of Nestorianism. Later, Cyril's council proceeded to condemn John of Antioch, but it did not depose him.

The council presided over by Cyril is the one which came to be accepted as the Third Ecumenical Council. It declared that Cyril's teaching concerning the Lord Jesus Christ was in harmony with the Nicene Creed, and it included in its decrees (a) Cyril's second Letter to Nestorius; and (b) A letter with twelve anathemas against Nestorianism produced by Cyril and the synod of Alexandria in 430, and sent to Nestorius in that year. This meant that the Council was giving its approval to the use of the word *theotokos* for the Blessed Virgin Mary. The Council declared that she did not give birth merely to a man with a human nature: her Son is the eternal Son of the Father, who took His human nature and flesh in her womb. She truly is the "God-bearing" Virgin!

The first of the twelve anathemas directed against Nestorianism concerns those who deny the truth concerning both Jesus and Mary:

> **If anyone will not confess that the Emmanuel is very God, and that therefore the Holy Virgin is the Mother of God (*theotokos*), inasmuch as in the flesh she bore the Word of God made flesh [as it is written "The Word was made flesh"]: let him be anathema.**

After the Council, John of Antioch changed his mind concerning Nestorianism and the use of *theotokos*, accepted the decrees of Cyril's council, produced a theological Statement now known as the Formula of Union, and made peace with Cyril, who accepted the Statement. The Formula of Union has been preserved in the decrees of the Council of Ephesus. Here it is:

> **We confess, therefore, our Lord Jesus Christ, the only begotten Son of God, perfect God and perfect man composed of a rational soul and a body, begotten before the ages from his Father in respect of his divinity, but likewise in these last days for us and for our salvation from Mary the Virgin in respect of his manhood; consubstantial with the Father in respect of his divinity and at the same time consubstantial with us in respect of his manhood. For a union of two natures has been accomplished. Hence we confess one Christ, one Son, one Lord. According to this understanding of the union without confusion, we confess the holy Virgin to be the Mother of God [Theotokos] because the divine Word became flesh and was made man and from the very conception united to himself the temple taken from her. As for the evangelical**

and apostolic statements about the Lord, we recognize that theologians employ some indifferently in view of the unity of person, but distinguish others in view of the duality of natures, applying the God-befitting ones to Christ's divinity and the lowly ones to his humanity.

Obviously, this declaration amounts to a definite rejection of the heresy associated with the name of Nestorius and a positive acceptance of the title of *Theotokos* ("God-bearer") for the Blessed Virgin Mary.

It is interesting to note that in terms of etymology the Latin equivalent of *Theotokos* is *Deipara;* but, in fact, the Latin expression generally used in the West to translate *Theotokos* was *Dei Genitrix* ("Mother of God"). Some modern translators— including those who translate the Orthodox Liturgy—seem to prefer not to translate *theotokos* into English but to render it as a title, "Theotokos," so that it effectively becomes an English word. Dr. Percival translates *theotokos* as "Mother of God" throughout his volume on the Councils and also provides a justification for doing so (*The Seven Councils*, p. 210).

THE COUNCIL OF CHALCEDON (451)

If Nestorius is the heretic uniquely associated with the Council of Ephesus, then Eutyches, an Archimandrite at a large monastery in Constantinople, is the heretic uniquely associated with the Council of Chalcedon. Eutyches denied that the manhood (human nature, humanity) of Jesus was consubstantial with ours; further, he also taught that while there were two natures before the union there was only one after the union in the one Person of Jesus Christ. So his theology became known as Monophysitism (from *monos,* one, and *physis*, nature).

At a Synod in Constantinople in August 449, which had been called by the Emperor Theodosius II, Eutyches was acquitted of heresy and restored to his monastery, from where he had been expelled the previous year as a heretic. This synod was later called "the Robber Council" because Pope Leo described it in a letter to the Empress Pulcheria in these words—*non iudicum, sed latrocinium* ("not a Just but a Robber Council").

The decisions of the *Latrocinium* were reversed by the Fourth Ecumenical Council, which was called by the Emperor Marcian and which met over the water from Constantinople in Chalcedon on October 8, 451. Included in its decrees is the Letter of Pope Leo to Flavian, Patriarch of Constantinople, about Eutyches and his heresy; the Letters of Cyril, Patriarch of Alexander, to Nestorius and to John, Patriarch of Antioch; and a Definition of the Faith and 29 Canons. The Definition accepts both the Creed of the 318 Fathers at Nicea and the Creed of 150 at Constantinople and stands opposed to all heresy—in particular to Nestorianism and Eutychianism. And it proceeds:

> **The Synod opposes those who would rend the mystery of the economy into a duad of Sons; and it banishes from the assembly of priests those who dare to say that the Godhead of the Only-begotten is passible; and it resists those who imagine a mixture or confusion of the two natures of Christ; and it drives away those who fancy that the form of a servant taken by him of us is of a heavenly or any other kind of being; and it anathematizes those who first idly talk of the natures of the Lord as "two before the union," and then conceive but one "after the union."**

We shall return to the heresies here rejected in our exposition in chapter eight.

The positive Definition of the Faith produced by the Bishops was in these terms:

> **Following, then, the holy fathers, we all with one voice teach that it should be confessed that our Lord Jesus Christ is one and the same Son, the same perfect in**

Godhead, the same perfect in manhood, truly God and truly man, the same consisting of a rational soul and body; consubstantial [*homoousios*] with the Father as to his Godhead, and the same consubstantial [*homoousios*] with us as to his manhood; in all things like unto us, sin only excepted; begotten of the Father before the ages as to his Godhead, and in the last days, the same, for us and for our salvation, of the Virgin Mary, Mother of God [*Theotokos*], as to his manhood;

One and the same Christ, Son, Lord, only-begotten, made known in two natures which exist without confusion, without change, without division, without separation; the difference of the natures having been in no wise taken away by reason of the union, but rather the properties of each being preserved, and both concurring into one Person [*prosopon*] and one Hypostasis—not parted or divided into two Persons [*prosopa*], but one and the same Son, only-begotten, the divine Word, the Lord Jesus Christ; even as the prophets from of old have spoken concerning him, and as the Lord Jesus Christ himself has taught us and the Creed of our Fathers has handed down.

These things, therefore, having been expressed by us with the greatest accuracy and attention, the holy Ecumenical Synod defines that no one shall be allowed to bring forth a different Faith, nor to write, nor to put together, nor to think, nor to teach it to others. But such as dare either to put together another faith, or to bring forward or to teach or to deliver a different Creed to such as wish to convert to the knowledge of the truth from the Gentiles, or Jews or any heresy whatever—if they be Bishops or clerics let them be deposed, the Bishops from the episcopate the clerics from the clergy; but if they be monks or laity, let them be anathematized.

We shall return to the study of this orthodox dogma of the Person of Christ in chapter nine below.

The Canons of this Council may be summarized in the following way:

1. Concerning keeping the Canons of previous synods.
2. Concerning Bishops who perform ordinations for money.
3. Concerning clergy who engage in business for financial gain.
4. Concerning monks who act against the wishes of the local bishop.
5. Concerning the transferring of a cleric from one diocese to another.
6. Concerning the necessity of a cleric to have a "title" when he is ordained.
7. Concerning clerics or monks who go back into the world.
8. Concerning clerics who are in charge of almshouses, monasteries and martyrs' shrines.
9. Concerning the duty of clerics not to go to a secular court but to the Bishops' court.
10. Concerning those clerics who are wrongly appointed to churches in two cities at the same time.
11. Concerning the supplying of ecclesiastical letters for travelers.
12. Concerning dividing one province into two so that there are two metropolitans.
13. Concerning foreign clerics without letters of commendation from their own Bishop.
14. Concerning the marriage of those in holy orders.
15. Concerning the age and behavior of deaconesses.
16. Concerning virgins and monks dedicated to God who contract a marriage.
17. Concerning the stability of dioceses.
18. Concerning the formation of secret societies for clerics or monks.
19. Concerning the need to have local synods regularly.

20. Concerning the transfer of a cleric from city to city.
21. Concerning the bringing of charges by clerics against Bishops.
22. Concerning the taking of the possessions of a deceased Bishop.
23. Concerning expelling unemployed foreign clerics and turbulent monks from Constantinople.
24. Concerning the error of turning monasteries into hostelries.
25. Concerning the length of time within which an ordination of a Bishop for a vacant diocese should occur.
26. Concerning the employment of an administrator by a Bishop.
27. Concerning the carrying off of girls into cohabitation.
28. Concerning the prerogatives of the Patriarchate of Constantinople.
29. Concerning the status of a Bishop who has been removed from his office.

To read these Canons and then to ponder them is to get a good grasp of some of the major disciplinary problems being faced by the Church at that time in the East.

It is worth remembering that even the prestige and authority of the Emperor along with the imperial bureaucracy could not cause and maintain the visible unity of the Church. After the Council of Ephesus a separate Church of Nestorian Christians, which has survived into the present as the Assyrian Christians, came into being; further, after the Council of Chalcedon separate Monophysite Churches (e.g., the Copts and Syrian Jacobites) began to exist which have also survived to the present day.

FOR FURTHER READING

Leo Donald Davis, S.J., *The First Seven Ecumenical Councils*, chaps. 4-5, provides a good account of the background to these two Councils, as does L'Huillier, *The Church of the Ancient Councils*. The texts in English are found in Henry R. Percival, *The Seven Ecumenical Councils*, chaps. 4-5. For the Greek and Latin texts see Norman P. Tanner, S.J., *Decrees of the Ecumenical Councils*, vol.1., pp. 37-104. A thorough study of the Fourth Council is R. V. Sellers, *The Council of Chalcedon* (London: SPCK, 1961). A good study of the Church history of this period is provided by W. H. C. Frend, *The Rise of Christianity* (Philadelphia: Fortress Press, 1984). An older book, which has many insights concerning the relation of the Emperors to the Church and of the Church to the culture, is Charles N. Cochrane, *Christianity and Classical Culture* (New York: Oxford University Press, 1944). Further, an essay which provides an excellent introduction to the role of Christianity in the Roman Empire is Christopher Dawson, "St. Augustine and his Age," in *St. Augustine* (New York: Meridian Books, 1957).

CHAPTER THREE

Constantinople II (553)
Constantinople III (681)
& Nicea II (787)

Where there is any interest at all in the history of the Early Church, the decrees of the first four Ecumenical Councils are generally reasonably well known. However, in contrast, those of the next three Councils are generally known only vaguely or in part. This state of affairs is understandable, since not only is the history surrounding them complicated by the relation of Church and State and rivalry between the Patriarchates, but also because the decrees of the fifth and sixth only make clearer what had been already taught by the Councils of Ephesus (431) and Chalcedon (451). Further, their reception in the West—at least initially—was very mixed. Then, it must be admitted that the decrees of the Seventh Council are of little interest to most Protestants. This is because they are not involved in their worship or devotions with the use of icons or the cult of the saints and so do not need guidance in this matter! Further, they are also of minimal interest to Roman Catholics since the subject of icons/images and decorative art was addressed with clarity by the Council of Trent in the sixteenth century (see Appendix III).

Our aim is to gain a general appreciation of these three councils, so that in later chapters we can understand both the content of the Catholic Faith with respect to the Person of Christ and the right use of icons in Christian worship and devotion.

THE SECOND COUNCIL OF CONSTANTINOPLE (553)

On May 5, 553, in the great hall next to the magnificent Cathedral of Hagia Sophia, the Council convened. Initially it had been called together at the agreement of the Emperor Justinian and Pope Vigilius, who was in exile from Rome in Constantinople. The president of the assembly was Eutychius, the Patriarch of Constantinople, and most of the 151 to 168 Bishops present were from the East. Vigilius did not attend but was in constant communication with the Council, which went along paths he did not favor. In particular, he did not agree with the formal anathematizing of three leading Antiochene theologians (Theodore of Mopsuestia [d. 428], Theodoret of Cyprus [d. 466] and Ibas of Edessa [d. 457]), who had actually died in the communion of the Catholic Church. Later, however, he was to change his mind and accept what the Council said and did concerning them.

Without the presence of the Bishop of Rome, the Council, seeking to please the Emperor and to finish its business, proceeded in its sentence against the three topics known as "The Three Chapters" (*ta tria kephalaia*) to condemn them and to anathematize their authors. ["The Three Chapters", already condemned by Justinian in an edict in 543-534, were (1) the person and works of Theodore of Mopsuestia; (2) the writings of Theodoret against Cyril of Alexandria, and (3) the letter of Ibas of Edessa to Maris. All three were considered to be sympathetic to, or exponents of, the heresy of Nestorianism.]

Towards the end of the lengthy "Sentence" the Bishops summarized their position:

Consequently we anathematize the aforesaid Three Chapters, that is the heretical Theodore of Mopsuestia along

with his detestable writings, and the heretical writings of Theodoret, and the heretical letter which Ibas is alleged to have written. We anathematize the supporters of these works and those who write or have written in defense of them, or who are bold enough to claim that they are orthodox, or who have defended or tried to defend their heresy in the names of the holy Fathers or of the holy Council of Chalcedon.

However, to make absolutely clear where they stood they also set forth fourteen anathemas. The first—a splendid statement of the Holy Trinity as both the ontological and economic Trinity—we shall quote in full. The next six teach the unity of the Person of Jesus Christ and pronounce anathemas on false teaching, while those that follow teach the duality of natures in the One Person and pronounce anathemas on false teaching. The heresies associated with the names of Arius, Apollinarius, Nestorius, Theodore and Eutyches are particularly in view in the condemnations.

Anathema 1

If anyone will not confess that the Father, the Son and the Holy Spirit have one nature or substance, that they have one power and authority, that there is a consubstantial Trinity, One Godhead to be adored in three Subsistences or Persons; let him be anathema.

There is only one God and Father, from whom all things come, and one Lord Jesus Christ through whom all things are, and one Holy Spirit, in whom all things are.

It is now generally agreed by scholars that the additional fifteen anathemas against doctrines of Origen of Alexandria and of Evagrius of Pontus (d. 399), often attributed to this Council, did not actually come from this Council. Therefore, we shall not discuss them here. (They may be read in Percival, *The Seven Councils*, pp. 318-19, and are discussed by Meyendorff, *Christ in Eastern Thought*, chap. 3.)

Finally, it is to be noted that this Council provided no canons on ecclesiastical discipline. Its sole concern was with doctrine. This was also the case at the next Ecumenical Council in Constantinople (for which see below). However, the Synod of Trullo (sometimes called "Quinisext" or "Fifth-Sixth"), which was summoned by the Emperor Justinian II in 692, produced 102 canons which have been regarded as equivalent to decrees of an ecumenical council in eastern canon law. (These 102 canons may be read in Percival, *The Seven Councils*, pp. 356-408.)

CONSTANTINOPLE III (680-681)

If the cause of the calling of the Sixth Ecumenical Council is to be put in one word it is "Monothelitism"—the heresy that there is only one will in the Incarnate Word, Jesus Christ. The Emperor, Constantine IV, instructed Patriarch George of Constantinople to call the Council, and it met on September 10, 680, in the imperial palace. Six months earlier a synod had met in Rome under Pope Agatho and had set forth a Confession of Faith, which included the rejection and condemnation of Monothelitism. This Statement was taken to Constantinople by the papal Legates to the Ecumenical Council and was influential in the process of the production of the "Exposition of the Faith" produced by the Council.

The central portion of this Confession is as follows:

> **Following the five holy Ecumenical Councils and the holy and approved Fathers, with one voice defining that our Lord Jesus Christ must be confessed to be very God and very man, one of the holy and consubstantial and life-giving Trinity, perfect in Deity and perfect in humanity, very God and very man, of a reasonable soul and human**

body subsisting; consubstantial with the Father as touching his Godhead and consubstantial with us as touching his manhood; in all things like unto us, sin only excepted; begotten of his Father before all ages according to his Godhead, but in these last days for us men and for our salvation made man of the Holy Ghost and of the Virgin Mary, strictly and properly the Mother of God according to the flesh; one and the same Christ our Lord, the only-begotten Son to be acknowledged of two natures which undergo no confusion, no change, no separation, no division, the peculiarities of neither nature being lost by the union, but rather the property of each nature being preserved, concurring in one Person and in one Subsistence, not parted or divided into two persons but one and the same only-begotten Son of God, the Word, our Lord Jesus Christ, according as the prophets of old have taught us and as our Lord Jesus Christ himself hath instructed us, and the Creed of the holy Fathers has delivered to us.

We likewise declare that in him are two natural wills and two natural operations which undergo no division, no change, no partition, no confusion, in accordance with the teaching of the holy Fathers. And these two natural wills are not opposed to each other (God forbid!) as the impious heretics assert, but his human will follows and that not as resisting and reluctant, but rather as subject to his divine and omnipotent will. For it was right that the flesh should be moved but subject to the divine will, according to the most wise Athanasius. For as his flesh is called and is the flesh of God the Word, so also the natural will of his flesh is called and is the proper will of God the Word, as he himself says: "I came down from heaven, not that I might do my own will but the will of the Father which sent me" where he calls his own will the will of his flesh, inasmuch as his flesh was also his own. For as his most holy and immaculate animated flesh was not destroyed because it was deified but continued in its own

43

state and nature [or "in its own limit and category"], so also his human will, although deified, was not suppressed, but was rather preserved according to the saying of Gregory the Theologian: "His will, when he is considered as Savior, is not contrary to God but is totally deified."

We glorify two natural operations in the same our Lord Jesus Christ our true God which undergo no division, no change, no partition, no confusion—that is to say a divine operation and a human operation, according to the divine preacher Leo, who most distinctly asserts: "For each form does in communion with the other what pertains properly to it, the Word, namely, doing that which pertains to the Word, and the flesh that which pertains to the flesh."

For we will not admit one natural operation in God and in the creature, as we will not exalt into the divine essence what is created, nor will we bring down the glory of the divine nature to the place suited to the creature.

We recognize the miracles and the suffering as of one and the same Person, but of one or the other nature of which he is and in which he exists, as Cyril admirably says. Preserving, therefore, the "no confusion" and "no division" we make this brief confession of faith: Believing our Lord Jesus Christ to be one of the Trinity and after the incarnation our true God, we say that his two natures shone forth in his one Subsistence in which he both performed the miracles and endured the sufferings through the whole of his providential dwelling here, and that not in appearance only but in very deed, and this by reason of the difference of nature which must be recognized in the same Person, for although joined together yet each nature wills and does the things proper to it and that without division and without confusion. Wherefore, we confess two wills and two operations, concurring most fitly in him for the salvation of the human race.

We shall reflect upon this theology of two wills in Christ in Chapter nine.

NICEA II (787)

The Empress Irene, acting as Regent for her son, Emperor Constantine VI (780-797), set in motion the events which led to the assembly of Bishops at Nicea in 787, which became the Seventh Ecumenical Council. Unlike her deceased husband and several emperors before him, she was wholly in favor of the artistic decoration of churches and the use of icons. She was an iconodule, not an iconoclast, and wished to reverse her husband's policy of removing and destroying holy pictures (icons). Her task was not easy since much of the army, some of the Bishops and many of the married clergy in the parishes were committed to Christian worship and piety without icons— put negatively, they were in favor of iconoclasm.

She intended that this Council would achieve two major purposes—(a) to condemn the decrees in support of iconoclasm passed by the Council of 338 Bishops held at Hieria and St. Mary of Blachernae in 754 (a Council which claimed to be the seventh ecumenical council), and (b) to restore unity to the Church which was divided over the issue of the legitimacy of the use of icons in churches, monasteries and homes.

Pope Hadrian I, Bishop of Rome, agreed to the calling of the Council. The Patriarch of Constantinople, Tarasius, informed the three eastern Patriarchs of Alexandria, Jerusalem and Antioch, and the assembly convened on August 1, 787, in the Basilica of the Holy Apostles in Constantinople. Its session was brief because soldiers, who supported the policy of iconoclasm, entered and brought the proceedings to a halt. The Empress, however, was determined that the Council would meet and achieve the ends she desired. So, with the cooperation of faithful soldiers, she moved the Bishops and Legates across the Bosphorus to Nicea, where they reassembled on September 24, 787, some 452 years after the First Ecumenical Council had met in the same place.

Having finished their work there, they were able to reassemble in Constantinople in the Magnaura Palace on October 23 in the presence of the Empress Irene and the Emperor Constantine VI, to approve the Definition (Decree) and Canons passed at Nicea. These documents made clear that the aims of the Empress were achieved; the use of icons was restored to the Church and the Bishop of Rome was again in communion with the Patriarchs of the East.

The Bishop of Rome was not present but represented by two legates. With Patriarch Tarasius they shared the presidency of the Council, whose membership varied between 258 and 335 Bishops and Legates (due in part to the reinstatement of iconoclast Bishops). The Definition of the Iconoclast Council of 754 was read and refuted point by point, line by line; an orthodox Definition, explaining the purpose and use of icons, was agreed upon and canons were promulgated.

The Definition of Nicea II (787) celebrates the providence of God in the assembly of the Council, accepts the previous six Ecumenical Councils, confesses the Creed of Constantinople (381), anathematizes all the major heretics, and defends all genuine, holy traditions whether written or unwritten (especially that of the production of representational art). Then it states:

> **To make our confession short we declare that we keep unchanged all the ecclesiastical traditions handed down to us, whether in writing or verbally, one of which is the making of pictorial representations, agreeable to the history of the preaching of the Gospel: a tradition useful in many respects, but especially in this, so that the Incarnation of the Word of God is shown forth as real and not merely imaginary, and brings us a similar benefit. For, things that mutually illustrate one another undoubtedly possess one another's message.**

We, therefore, following the royal pathway and the divinely inspired authority of our holy Fathers and the traditions of the Catholic Church (for, as we all know, the Holy Spirit indwells her), define with full precision and accuracy that just as the figure of the precious and life-giving Cross, so also the venerable and holy pictures (*eikonas*), as well in painting and mosaic as in other fit materials, should be set forth in the holy churches of God, and on the sacred vessels and on the vestments and on the hangings and in the pictures *(sanisin)* both in houses and by the wayside, namely, the picture *(eikon)* of our Lord and Savior Jesus Christ, of our spotless Lady *(despoines)* the holy Mother of God *(theotokos)*, of the honorable angels, of all holy and pious men.

For the more frequently they are seen in artistic representation the more readily are men lifted up to the memory of, and the longing after, their prototypes; and to these should be given salutation and honorable reverence *(aspasmon kai timetiken proskunesin)*, not indeed the true worship *(latreian)* which is fitting *(prepei)* for the Divine nature alone; but to these, as to the figure *(tupo)* of the holy and life-giving Cross, and to the holy Gospels, and to the other sacred objects, incense and lights may be offered according to ancient pious custom. For the honor which is paid to the picture *(eikon)* passes on to that which the picture represents, and he who reveres *(proskunon)* the picture reveres in it the subject represented.

So it is that the teaching of our holy fathers, that is, the Tradition of the Catholic Church, which from one end of the earth to the other has received the Gospel, is strengthened. And so it is that we follow Paul, who spoke in Christ, and the entire, divine apostolic company and the holy fathers, holding fast the traditions which we have received. So we sing prophetically the triumphal hymns of the Church: "Rejoice greatly, O daughter of Zion; shout,

O daughter of Jerusalem: rejoice and be glad with all thine heart. The Lord hath taken away from thee the oppression of thine enemies. The Lord is a King in the midst of thee; thou shalt not see evil any more, and peace shall be unto thee for ever [Zeph. 3:14-15, Septuagint]."

Those, therefore, who dare to think or teach otherwise, or who follow the wicked heretics to spurn the traditions of the Church and to invent some novelty, or who reject some of those things which the Church has received (e.g., the Book of the Gospels, or the image of the Cross, or the pictorial icons, or the holy relics of a martyr), or who devise perverted and evil prejudices against cherishing the lawful traditions of the Catholic Church, or who turn to common uses the sacred vessels of the venerable monasteries, we command that they be deposed if they be Bishops or Clerics and excommunicated if they be monks or lay people.

ANATHEMAS CONCERNING THE HOLY ICONS

If anyone does not confess that Christ our God can be represented in his humanity, let him be anathema.

If anyone does not accept artistic representation of evangelical scenes, let him be anathema.

If anyone does not salute such representations as standing for the Lord and his saints, let him be anathema.

If anyone rejects any written or unwritten tradition of the Church, let him be anathema.

In the final part of this book, we shall return to reflect upon the theology of this Definition, which, regrettably, because of inaccurate translations into Latin, was misunderstood and misrepresented in the West for a long time.

Those who formulated the Definition and who opposed iconoclasm did so at least in part for theological reasons. They were wholly committed to the Chalcedonian doctrine that the Word of God became Man, with real manhood. Thus as Man he could be presented in an art form. Their opponents tended towards or were committed to Monophysitism, saw the manhood as temporary and partial, and thus were opposed to representations of real and full manhood on icons.

The twenty-two Canons of Nicea II were intended to establish the rightful freedom of the Church in spiritual matters, and to bring discipline and good order back into the Church after the disturbances caused by the Iconoclast controversies in the East and the collapse of the Empire in the West. Here is a brief summary of their contents.

1. Church canons exist to be observed by all clergy.
2. A Priest should only be ordained a Bishop if he agrees to keep the canons.
3. Secular rulers ought not to elect Bishops.
4. Bishops should not accept gifts in exchange for favors.
5. Clergy who disparage fellow clergy, who were appointed without distributing gifts, are subject to penalties.
6. Local synods are to be held each year.
7. Any church consecrated without the installation of holy relics is to have this defect made good.
8. Jews should only be received into the Church if they are genuine converts.
9. Books commending or supporting iconoclasm are to be handed in.
10. Clergy must not change dioceses without the agreement of the Bishop(s).
11. There should be administrators in episcopal houses and monasteries.

12. A Bishop or monastic Superior is to be a faithful steward of property.
13. To turn a monastery into a public inn is a sin.
14. Only those ordained should read from the ambo in church services.
15. A clergyman should not be appointed to office in two churches at the same time.
16. Clergy should not wear expensive clothing.
17. A monk should not attempt to found a house of prayer unless he has adequate funding.
18. Women should not live in the houses of Bishops or in male monasteries.
19. Candidates to be priests, monks or nuns are to be accepted without the presentation of gifts.
20. No more double monasteries (monks and nuns) are to be started.
21. Monks ought not to transfer from one monastery to another without permission.
22. Monks should always say grace and act with propriety when eating in public and in the company of women.

As we have noted with other Canons, these provide indications of the kinds of tensions and problems being faced by the Church, especially in the East.

The decrees of this Council were not immediately received by all parts of the Church. It took a long time and much controversy and strife before iconoclasm ceased to be an important movement in the East. The Feast of Orthodoxy was established in the East in 842 to celebrate the final downfall of the Iconoclastic party and the full restoration of icons. Celebrated on the First Sunday in Lent, this Feast became the joyous commemoration of the orthodox, true and right Faith and its victory by the grace of the Holy Trinity over all heresies.

FOR FURTHER READING

For the historical background to each of the three Councils see Leo Donald Davis, S.J., *The First Seven Ecumenical Councils*, chaps. 6-8, and L'Huillier, *The Church of the Ancient Councils*. For the texts in English see H. R. Percival, *The Seven Ecumenical Councils,* chaps. 6-10; and for the texts in Greek and Latin see Norman P. Tanner, S.J., *Decrees of the Ecumenical Councils*, vol. 1, pp. 105-56. For the history of the Church in this period see H. Jedin, ed., *History of the Church*, vol. 2 (New York: Herder, 1980). There is much that is helpful for the understanding of the controversies over Icons in John Meyendorff, *Christ in Eastern Thought* (Crestwood, NY: St. Vladimir's Press, 1975), especially chap. 9, and in Jaroslav Pelikan, *The Spirit of Eastern Christendom (600-1700)* (Chicago: University of Chicago Press, 1974), chap. 3. See also Paul Evdokimov, *The Art of the Icon: A Theology of Beauty* (Redondo Beach, CA: Oakwood Publications, 1990).

PART TWO:

THE HOLY TRINITY

Our Father, who art in heaven, hallowed be thy Name. Thy
kingdom come. Thy will be done on earth as it is in heaven.
Give us this day our daily bread. And forgive us our trespasses, as we forgive those who trespass against us. And
lead us not into temptation, but deliver us from the Evil One.
For Thine is the kingdom and the power and the glory of the
Father, and of the Son, and of the Holy Spirit, now, and ever,
and unto ages of ages.

The Lord's Prayer, Orthodox Liturgy

Blessed is the kingdom of the Father, and of the Son, and of
the Holy Spirit, now, and ever, and unto ages of ages.

Liturgy of the Catechumens, Orthodox Church

CHAPTER FOUR

From the Father through the Son and in the Holy Spirit

It is very difficult if not impossible for us to place ourselves alongside the Fathers of the early Church and read the Bible exactly as they actually read it. Therefore, in this chapter I shall not attempt to enter the minds of the Fathers to explain the way they read, studied and meditated upon the books of the Bible. However, I shall first make some preliminary remarks to provide a context in which to look at the biblical evidence.

First of all, and of fundamental importance, is that the early Church was self-consciously Trinitarian in that all baptisms from the earliest times were "in the name of the Father and of the Son and of the Holy Spirit." These words of Jesus did not specifically state the exact ontological or metaphysical relation of the Son and the Holy Spirit to the Father, but they did place the Three together in an inseparable way. So the Church spoke of the Holy Triad or the Holy Trinity from the earliest times. Yet, while speaking of the Triad, they clearly believed that "the God" was not "the Godhead" but "the Father of our Lord Jesus Christ." The belief in Yahweh (= Jehovah or the LORD) inherited from the Jews and proclaimed in the holy pages of the Bible was in Christian terms belief in "the Father Almighty." And this Yahweh, the One God and the Father, was the God who has both an Only-begotten Son, Jesus Christ, and a Holy Spirit, who proceeds from him and rests upon his Son.

Secondly, in the worship of the local churches and in private devotion, prayers were addressed to Jesus the Lord. This both assumed and raised the question as to his divinity. And the question, given the conviction that Yahweh, the One God, is the Father, was itself a question of the relation of Jesus Christ to the Father. Jesus can only be God if he has an eternal relation to the Father, in and by which the Father's deity is communicated to him. The metaphysical question arose out of the apparently simple form of Christian prayer and worship. And the same question arose in other contexts as well—e.g., when Christians explained their Faith to Jews and to pagans and when they claimed that through Jesus Christ alone they received the salvation of God. What Christians were saying in effect was that the answer to the question "Who is God?" is intimately and inextricably related to the questions "Who is Jesus?" and "What is the exact relation of Jesus to the One he called the Father?"

What I shall attempt to do in this chapter is to gather together and present the basic scriptural evidence for belief in the Holy Triad. My purpose is to give my reader sufficient grasp of the biblical teaching that he can appreciate the doctrinal debates and conclusions reached in the patristic period concerning the relation of both the Son and the Holy Spirit to the Father. And what I present is not in the patristic sense, strictly speaking, theology (= the contemplative study of the Holy Trinity in terms of the inner relations of the Three), but the economy of God (= the activity of the Father with his Son and his Spirit in the creation and redemption of the world). In modern terminology, I present the "economic Trinity" of the sacred Scriptures not the "ontological Trinity" (= "the immanent Trinity") of holy Dogma. In Revelation, of course, the latter is only known through the former.

(i) Creation

The Old Testament makes it clear that Yahweh is the Creator of the heavens and the earth (Gen. 1-3; Is. 42:5). He creates and sustains the cosmos by his creative word/wisdom and his powerful breath or Spirit:

> By the word of Yahweh were the heavens made;
> And all their host by the breath of his mouth (Ps. 33:6).

Three New Testament writers build upon this teaching concerning the word and wisdom of Yahweh—which in the Old Testament is found in both the canonical and deutero-canonical books of the Septuagint—as they develop their Christology. For them, Jesus is the personal Word and Wisdom of God.

First of all, in the Prologue of the Gospel of John there are these statements:

> In the beginning was the Word, and the Word was with God, and the Word was God. He was in the beginning with God; all things were made through him, and without him was not anything made that was made (1:1-3).

The whole of creation is included in one broad sweep, as it is said that the Father created *through* (not "by") the Word, who is the Son.

In the second place, in Paul's Letter to the church in Colossae there is this teaching:

> For in him [the Lord Jesus Christ, the beloved Son] all things were created, in heaven and on earth, visible and invisible, whether thrones or dominions or principalities or powers; all things have been created through him and unto him. He is before all things, and in him all things hold together (1:16-17).

By the prepositions *in* and *through,* Paul communicates the agency and participation of the Son in the creation of heaven and earth. In another place, Paul presents the activity of Christ in the sustaining and maintaining of the creation: "There is one Lord, Jesus Christ, through whom are all things and through whom we exist" (1 Cor. 8:6). Further, God's plan is "for the fullness of time to unite all things in him [Christ], things in heaven and things on earth" (Eph. 1:10). Here the movement is towards God, what shall be when Christ's redeeming work is totally completed.

Finally, the writer of the Letter to the Hebrews, making use of description of Wisdom in the Septuagint (the Greek version of the Hebrew Bible), wrote:

> In these last days God has spoken to us by a Son, whom he appointed the heir of all things, through whom also he created the world. He reflects the glory of God and bears the very stamp of his nature, upholding the universe by his word of power (1:2-3).

Here Christ is presented as active with the Father in both the creating (*through* him) and the upholding of the universe.

In none of these texts is there a mention of the Holy Spirit. However, it is surely right to assume that his presence and activity were taken for granted. For the first Christians the biblical (O.T.) teaching concerning the Spirit's activity in creation was revealed by God and could not be set aside. Thus the Father through the Son [the Word] and by the Holy Spirit [the breath of his mouth] is the Creator and Sustainer of the universe.

(ii) Salvation provided

Under the old covenant, Yahweh, the LORD, descended into his creation in a variety of ways—e.g., in theophanies, by sending angels and by placing his word in the mouths of prophets and sages. The new covenant was established to replace the old (a) by the descent and incarnation of the Word, who is the Son of the Father, and (b) by the descent of the Holy Spirit, sent by the Father and by his Son. Salvation, which presupposes the created order and thus occurs within creation, is from the Father, through the Son and by the Spirit.

The narratives of the conception and birth of Jesus in Luke's Gospel assume and proclaim that God sent his own Son to become man; to achieve this miracle of Incarnation he sent his own Spirit to Mary so that she could and would conceive Jesus. The message is clear—Yahweh is active as Creator again, creating a new epoch, order and creation through his Son, who is Immanuel, and by his Spirit, the Life-Giver.

At the beginning of his second book, the Acts of the Apostles, Luke presents the descent of the Holy Spirit upon the assembled apostles and disciples. Now the new creation is beginning to take practical shape. The Son has descended and ascended and he has poured out his Spirit, who is the Spirit of the Father, upon his own disciples. Through this anointing and indwelling Spirit, the Lord Jesus will always be with his disciples on earth until the end of the age; and salvation from God in his name will be proclaimed throughout the world.

Speaking of the descent of the Son, St. Paul wrote: "When the time had fully come, God sent forth his Son, born of a woman, born under the law, to redeem those who were under the law..." (Gal. 4:4-5). Here is Incarnation to achieve redemption. The Lord Jesus Christ who was "rich" (in heavenly glory) for the sake of man and his salvation became "poor" (in earthly humiliation) so that, through his poverty, poor sinners might become rich (I Cor. 8:9). The descent of the Son from the heaven of heavens into the world of sin and shame, followed by his glorious exaltation back to the heaven of heavens, is powerfully dramatized by Paul in Philippians 2:5-11. Here the Son sets aside his eternal privileges and position with the Father and descends into the evil world for the salvation of mankind. To achieve this, he becomes a servant and dies on a cross.

In his Letters, Paul assumes that the Holy Spirit has descended and is present as the Spirit of Christ in the churches and within individual lives. He is present because many are confessing "Jesus is Lord," and this is only possible by the Spirit (I Cor. 12:3). Evidence of spiritual gifts given by the exalted Lord through the Spirit abound in the congregations (I Cor. 12). Believers know that God has sent the Holy Spirit for they experience the Spirit of the Father and the Son in their hearts as they cry out, "Abba, Father" (Gal. 4:6). In his own ministry as he proclaimed "Christ and him crucified," Paul knew that his speech was "in demonstration of the Spirit and power" and not in the wisdom of men (I Cor. 2:1-5).

For the apostle to the Gentiles, the work of salvation was the work of the Father and of his Son and of his Spirit. As he explained to Titus, his son in the Faith: "When the goodness and loving kindness of God [the Father] our Savior appeared, he saved us, not because of deeds done by us in righteousness, but in virtue of his own mercy, by the washing of regeneration and renewal in the Holy Spirit, which he poured out upon us richly through Jesus Christ our Savior" (Tit. 3:4-6).

At the beginning of his Letters, Paul usually wrote, "Grace to you and peace from God our Father and the Lord Jesus Christ" (e.g., Rom. 1:7). This is the downward movement from God the Father and from (through) his Son. The presence and work of the Holy Spirit is not stated but is assumed—by the presence and activity of the Holy Spirit, grace and peace become realities in the souls of believers.

Caught up in prayerful adoration of the Holy Trinity, Paul wrote these words at the beginning of the Letter to Ephesus:

> Blessed be the God and Father of our Lord Jesus Christ, who has blessed us in Christ with every spiritual blessing in the heavenly places, even as he chose us in him before the foundation of the world, that we should be holy and blame-

less before him. He destined us in love to be his sons through Jesus Christ, according to the purpose of his will, to the praise of his glorious grace which he freely bestowed upon us in the Beloved [Son]. In him we have redemption through his blood, the forgiveness of our trespasses, according to the riches of his grace which he lavished upon us (1:3-7).

He continued by blessing God because "you were sealed with the promised Holy Spirit, which is the guarantee of our inheritance until we acquire possession of it" (1:8-14).

The gracious, saving work of God in space and time is traced back here, as Paul engages in holy contemplation, to the purposes of the Father before the creation of the world. Yet the movement for the salvation of man is the same as elsewhere in Paul's writings—the Father (in his transcendent, eternal glory) through the Son (by the shedding of his blood) and by the Holy Spirit (the living guarantee of the fullness of the life of the age to come).

The Prologue to the Gospel of John declares that the Word, who is the only Son, comes into the world from the Father and that grace and truth (salvation and revelation) come through him. As Incarnate God, he is "the Lamb of God who takes away the sin of the world" (1:29). And in the much quoted words of John 3:16-17: "For God [the Father] so loved the world that he gave his only Son, that whoever believes in him should not perish but have eternal life. For God sent the Son into the world not to condemn the world, but that the world might be saved through him."

The sending and giving of the Spirit by the Father and the glorified Son to the disciples is given much emphasis in John 14-16. The Paraclete comes from the Father in the name of the Son: he brings the virtues of the Son to the disciples and continues the mission of the Son in the hostile world. Yet already in John 3:1-8 it was made clear that the same Spirit, who alone causes spiritual birth into the kingdom of God, is the Holy Spirit who is "from above," that is from the Father. There is salvation only for those who believe in the Son and are "born of the Spirit" and thus "born from above."

In I John, it is made clear that the fellowship of Christians is not only with each other "but is with the Father and the Son;" further, this is because they have "an anointing from the Holy One" which abides in them.

> By this we know that we abide in him [God] and he in us, because he has given us of his Spirit. And we have seen and testify that the Father has sent his Son as the Savior of the world. Whoever confesses that Jesus is the Son of God, God abides in him, and he in God. So we know and believe the love God has for us (4:13-16).

God the Father sent his Son into the world and gives his Spirit to those who believe in his Son in order that they may abide in God.

The same movement from the Father, through the Son and in the Holy Spirit may be seen in the rest of the books of the New Testament. In fact, it may be claimed that one unifying theme either implicit or explicit in all the books is that of the economic Trinity.

(iii) Salvation received

The four Gospels were not written merely to provide information concerning Jesus and satisfy curiosity as to his identity. They were written with an evangelistic purpose—to declare the Gospel of the Father concerning his Son, Jesus Christ, so that Jew and Gentile would believe in Jesus as Lord and Christ and in believing receive God's salvation. The purpose of the Gospels is to cause men to turn from sin and idolatry to trust, serve and worship the Father through his Son and by his Spirit. So while they certainly assume and powerfully declare the economic Trinity, practically speaking they were written to make the movement towards God the Father possible by providing the content of the good news of Jesus, in and by whom alone men know and come to the Father. In fact, we could say that everything in the New Testament was written in order to make possible the "Ascent" from earth into the "new heaven and earth," and from this evil age into the glorious age of the kingdom of God.

To be saved by God the Father into his everlasting kingdom of grace, it is necessary to be united in the Holy Spirit to Jesus Christ and be presented or brought to the Father by this divine agency. Such a removal out of sin into friendship with God is stated with clarity and power in the Letter to Ephesus, where the apostle is discussing the unity of Jew and Gentile in Christ and before God:

> Now in Christ Jesus you who once were far off have been brought near [to God] in the blood of Christ. For he is our peace, who has made us [Jew and Gentile] both one, and has broken down the dividing wall of hostility...that he might create in himself one new man in place of the two, so making peace, and might reconcile us to God in one body through the Cross, thereby bringing the hostility to an end. And he came and preached peace to you who were far off and peace to those who were near; for through him we have access in one Spirit to the Father (2:13-18).

The last words are very important: "Through Christ we have access in One Spirit to the Father." Here is the basis of both salvation and worship. Then he continues:

> So then you are no longer strangers and sojourners, but you are fellow citizens with the saints and members of the household of God, built upon the foundation of the apostles and prophets, Christ Jesus himself being the chief cornerstone, in whom the whole structure is joined together and grows into a holy temple to the Lord, in whom you also are built into it for a dwelling place of God in the Spirit (2:19-22).

Here is a powerful picture of a living temple centered on Christ, indwelt by the Holy Spirit and made not of stones of granite but of apostles, prophets and all true believers, both Jews and Gentiles. The temple rises from earth towards heaven, which is its goal. This divine household is built upon the saving work of Jesus Christ, energized and indwelt by the Holy Spirit, who is the Spirit of Christ, and is oriented towards the Father, who draws it to himself.

The Letter to the Hebrews contrasts that to which the Israelites were brought by the old Exodus through the Red Sea with that to which Christians are brought through the new Exodus of the Cross and Resurrection of Jesus.

> For you have not come to what may be touched, a blazing fire, and darkness, and gloom, and a tempest, and the sound of a trumpet, and a voice whose words made the hearers entreat that no further messages be spoken to them. For they could not endure the order that was given. "If even a beast touches the mountain it shall be stoned." Indeed, so terrifying was the sight that Moses said, "I tremble with fear." (12:18-21)

The writer is recalling what is recorded in Exodus 19 and Deuteronomy 9. He continues:

> But you have come to Mount Zion and to the city of the living God, the heavenly Jerusalem, and to innumerable angels in festal gathering, and to the assembly of the first-born who are enrolled in heaven, and to a judge who is God of all, and to the spirits of just men made perfect, and to Jesus, the mediator of the new covenant, and to the sprinkled blood that speaks more graciously than the blood of Abel (12:22-24).

Entry into the new creation is clearly only possible because of the sacrifice of Jesus Christ, who is the Mediator of the new covenant.

> For Christ has entered...into heaven itself, now to appear in
> the presence of God on our behalf (9:24).

Knowing through the Gospel what the Father through the Son
and in the Holy Spirit has done in establishing the new covenant, Christians are to respond wholeheartedly. Because they
know that the way to God is now wide open unto those who
believe the good news, they are to respond in worship and service.

> Therefore, brethren, since we have confidence to enter the
> sanctuary by the blood of Jesus, by the new and living way
> which he opened for us through the curtain, that is through
> his flesh, and since we have a great high priest over the house
> of God, let us draw near with a true heart in full assurance of
> faith, with our hearts sprinkled clean from an evil conscience
> and our bodies washed with pure water (10:19-22).

And in terms of practice:

> Let us hold fast the confession of our faith without waver-
> ing, for he [the Father] who promised is faithful; and let us
> consider how to stir up one another to love and to good works,
> not neglecting to meet together, as is the habit of some, but
> encouraging one another, and all the more as you see the
> Day drawing near (10:23-25).

As they wait for the Parousia of Christ, the Day of the Lord,
Christians are to ascend to the Father in spiritual communion
by offering him the sacrifice of good works and the corporate
activity of spiritual worship.

(iv) Worship as response

Salvation has three tenses in the New Testament. By the unique,
sacrificial, atoning death of Jesus Christ, salvation is procured

once for all and forever. We are saved by the propitiatory and expiatory death of the Lord Jesus. Once a person believes in Jesus and confesses that he is Lord, then he enters into salvation—he is being saved from sin and into the life of the Holy Trinity. Salvation is for him "already" experienced, but it is "not yet" fully realized. He knows that he is still a sinner in a mortal, sinful body. However, he will certainly enjoy the fullness of salvation when, after the Parousia of the Lord Jesus Christ, in his resurrection body and with all the saints he beholds the glory of God the Father in the face of Jesus Christ in the power of the Holy Spirit.

The New Testament has a lot to say about the privileges and duties of those who are being saved from this evil age into the fullness of salvation in the life of the age to come. Within these privileges and duties we find worship and prayer. In such holy activities, the Church on earth is united in the Holy Spirit with the Lord Jesus Christ, Son of the Father and High Priest in heaven: her worship ascends to the Father within the worship and prayer offered unceasingly by Jesus, the Priest, to the Father. Christ at the right hand of the Father, interceding for his Church: and the Holy Spirit is interceding from within the souls of his people (Rom. 8:26, 34.). This activity of the Spirit with the Son to the Father for the elect will continue until the end of the age when Christ shall come again to judge the living and the dead.

Speaking as a Christian to Christian believers, Paul told the church in Philippi: "We are the true circumcision who worship God in spirit, [or "worship by the Spirit of God"] and glory in Christ Jesus and put no confidence in the flesh" (3:3). Here is Paul's simple theology. Because of Jesus Christ (who he is and what he has done and is doing), worship ascends in the Spirit to the Father.

Worship [Prayer] is not only thanksgiving, praise and worship; it can also be petition and intercession. Thus Paul made this request of the church in Rome, a church he had not yet visited: "I appeal to you, brethren, by our Lord Jesus Christ and by the love of the Spirit, to strive together with me in your prayers to God on my behalf, that I may be delivered from the unbelievers in Judea, and that my service for Jerusalem may be acceptable to the saints, so that by God's [the Father's] will I may come to you with joy and be refreshed in your company. The God of peace be with you all. Amen" (15:30-33).

In writing to the church in Colossae, Paul put it simply: "Whatever you do, in word or deed, do everything in the name of the Lord Jesus, giving thanks to the Father through him" (3:17). Likewise he told the church in Rome: "I appeal to you therefore, by the mercies of God, to present your bodies as a living sacrifice, holy and acceptable to God, which is your spiritual worship" (12:1).

The First Letter of Peter is clear that, as those who are chosen by the Father, redeemed by the precious blood of Christ and being sanctified by the Holy Spirit (1:1-2, 19), Christians are placed in such a privileged relation to God that they have a joyous duty both to proclaim the Gospel and offer spiritual sacrifice in worship and service:

> You are a chosen race, a royal priesthood, a holy nation, God's [the Father's] own people, that you may declare the wonderful deeds of him who called you out of darkness into his marvelous light. Once you were no people but now you are God's people; once you had not received mercy but now you have received mercy (2:9-10).

And recalling Psalm 118:22 and Isaiah 28:16, which refer to Christ as the chief cornerstone of God's new Temple, Peter wrote:

> Come to him, to that living stone, rejected by men but in God's [the Father's] sight chosen and precious; and like living stones be yourselves built up into a spiritual house to be

67

a holy priesthood, to offer spiritual sacrifices acceptable to God [the Father] through Jesus Christ (2:4-5).

The assembled local church, as the holy priesthood, offers its worship, prayer and service in the Holy Spirit to the Father through Christ the High Priest.

In his very short Letter Jude told his fellow Christians, whom he addressed as "those who are called, beloved in God the Father and kept for Jesus Christ," to "Build yourselves up on your most holy faith; pray in the Spirit; wait for the mercy of our Lord Jesus Christ unto eternal life." He ended the Letter with this doxology which points to the "Ascent" of the faithful to the Father.

> Now to him who is able to keep you from falling and to present you without blemish before the presence of his glory with rejoicing, to the only God, our Savior through Jesus Christ our Lord, be glory, majesty, dominion, and authority, before all time and now and forever. *Amen.*

So the Church, the Bride of Christ, invokes her Lord, giving him the honor which is his due, and moves in, with and through him to render her worship to the eternal Father. In this movement from earth to heaven, and from forgiven sinners to the heavenly Father, the Holy Spirit is wholly present, but invisible and often anonymous. Thus in the New Testament there is no example of prayer being offered directly to the Holy Spirit. This practice came later, after the dogma of the Trinity had been clarified and the divine personhood of the Holy Spirit clearly established as a truth of the Faith at the Council of Constantinople (381).

Even so, in Christian liturgy and devotion, direct addressing of the Holy Spirit is rare. The Father is made known to the Church through the Son and the Son is made known by the Spirit. However, there is no fourth divine Person to make the Spirit known. The Holy Spirit is the locus, even as the Son is the agent, rather than the object of divine revelation. Creation is from the Father, through the Son and in the Spirit, and the response of the creature is to the Father, through the Son and in the Spirit. Thus the Spirit is experienced within the Church rather like the air that is breathed. He is known in his effects and not like a visible, external object.

From this brief presentation of the Trinity in the economy, it is possible to see how and why controversy could arise concerning the status of the Son and of the Holy Spirit. It is clear that "God" is "the Father" and "the Father" is "God." However, it is not absolutely clear in what sense the incarnate Son, who is called "Lord," actually possesses and participates in the Godhead. To be pre-existent is one thing; but to be "God" is another. All agreed that the Son is pre-existent. Yet this does not settle the nature of his unique relation to the Father. Further, it is even less clear in what sense the Holy Spirit, who is also clearly pre-existent, is to be called God, or is to be said to possess the Godhead of the Father. So, though Baptism was in the Name of the Father, and the Son and the Holy Spirit, there was still room for debate as to the precise relations of the Three, one to another before and after the creation of space and time.

FOR FURTHER READING

For studies of the doctrine of the economic Trinity see A. W. Wainwright, *The Trinity in the New Testament* (London: SPCK, 1965) and Peter Toon, *Our Triune God: A Biblical Portrayal of the Trinity* (Wheaton, IL: Victor Books, 1996). For the dogma of the Trinity see Bertrand de Margerie, S.J., *The Christian Trinity in History* (Still River, MA: St. Bede's Publications, 1982).

CHAPTER FIVE

Arianism Rejected

It has been said, that a person has first to be a Christian to become a heretic, and that there has to be truth before there is heresy and error. In the early Church, the truth of the Gospel was known, believed, taught and preached before it was formally stated by synods of bishops in Ecumenical Councils. Thus, heresy existed from the apostolic age through to the first Council in 325. Not only the books of the New Testament, but also the writings of the early Fathers confirm this. For example, in the latter part of the second century, Irenaeus wrote a book against false knowledge, which is known in English through the translation of its Latin (not original Greek) title, *Against Heresies*.

ORIGINAL ARIANISM

The specific teaching, which was declared to be a heresy at the Council of Nicea in 325, is known as Arianism, after Arius, a presbyter of the church in Alexandria in Egypt. Arius and others who supported him were influenced by the teaching of Lucian, who ran a theological school in Antioch, and to whom they were exceedingly loyal. Lucian was absolutely clear that there is one and one only God, who is both the God of the Old Testament and the God of Jesus Christ. This Antiochene theologian was a Unitarian in contrast to a Trinitarian, since he taught that there is no plurality within the unity of God. Further, he held that the Logos, incarnate as Jesus, is a supremely unique, created being, who is supernatural but not divine in the sense that the Father is divine.

Commenting on the origins of the Arian controversy, Dr. J. N. D. Kelly, wrote:

> The outbreak of the Arian debate is probably to be placed somewhere in 318, when Arius was presiding as priest over the church of Baucalis. The broad lines of his system, which was a model of dovetailed logic, are not in any doubt. Its keystone was the conviction of the absolute transcendence and perfection of the Godhead. God (and it was God the Father whom he had in mind) was absolutely one: there could be no other God in the proper sense of the word beside him. (*Early Christian Creeds*, p. 232.)

Arius explained his own theology to his Bishop, Alexander, in a letter sent about 320 from a refuge outside the city. His clear belief in the absolute unity of God and the distinctiveness of the Son as a unique creature cannot be missed:

> We acknowledge One God, alone unbegotten, alone everlasting, alone unbegun, alone true, alone having immortality, alone wise, alone good, alone sovereign: judge, governor and administrator of all, unalterable and unchangeable, just and good, God of Law and Prophets and New Testament; who begat an Only-begotten Son before eternal times, through whom he has made both the ages and the universe; and begat him not in semblance, but in truth: and that he made him subsist at his own will, unalterable and unchangeable; perfect creature of God, but not as one of the creatures; offspring, but not as one of things that have come into existence... (*A New Eusebius*, p. 346.)

To establish his own orthodoxy, Arius proceeded to declare that he rejected the teaching of the heretics Valentinus, Manichaeus and Sabellius. In doing this, he rejected the use of the (soon to be famous) word, *homoousios*, of the Son, since he believed that it implied that (as used by Manichaeus and others) the Son is an actual portion or piece of the Father and thus, there is actual division within the divine essence (*ousia*) of the Godhead.

About the same time, Arius also wrote a letter to Eusebius, Bishop of Nicomedia, his friend and former fellow student in the academy of Lucian in Antioch. He said:

> I want to tell you that the Bishop [of Alexandria] makes great havoc of us and persecutes us severely, and is in full sail against us: he has driven us out of the city as atheists, because we do not concur in what he publicly preaches, namely, that, "God has always been, and the Son has always been: the Father and the Son exist together: the Son has his existence unbegotten along with God ever being begotten, without having been begotten: God does not precede the Son by thought or by any interval however small: God has always been, the Son has always been: the Son is from God himself. (*Ibid.*, p. 344.)

Apparently, the Bishop's teaching that the Son is as eternal as is the Father and also that he is of the same deity as the Father, was heard by Arius and others as meaning that the Son is an actual part of the Father—and God who is indivisible is now divisible. His own position was:

> That the Son is not unbegotten, nor in any way part of the unbegotten; nor from some lower essence (i.e., from matter); but that by the Father's will and counsel he has subsisted before time and before ages as God full of grace and truth, only-begotten, unchangeable. And that he was not, before he was begotten, or created, or purposed, or established. For he was not unbegotten. (*Ibid.*, p. 345.)

73

Arius proceeded in his self-defense to explain to Eusebius the real cause of their persecution in Alexandria and Egypt:

> We are persecuted because we say, 'the Son had a beginning, but God is without beginning.' This is really the cause of our persecution; and, likewise, because we say that he is from nothing. And this we say because he is neither part of God, nor of a lower essence. (*Ibid.*, p. 345.)

Certainly, Arius clearly identified the basis of the bitter division. His Bishop said that the Son is not a creature, not even the highest possible form of a created being, because he is divine in the same way that the Father is divine. In contrast, Arius wanted to give the highest possible place to the Logos/Son in the divine scheme of things, but without stating that the Son possesses deity as the Father possesses deity.

Some of the theological sayings of Arius from his book, *Thalia* (= "Banquet," a popular medley of verse and prose), were collected by Athanasius and included in his own book, *On the Synods of Ariminum and Seleucia*. Here is a selection of them:

> We praise him [the Father] as without beginning, because of him [the Son] who has a beginning.

> For the Son is not equal, no, nor one in essence [homoousios] with the Father.

> At God's will, the Son is what and whatsoever he is. And when and since he was, from then he has subsisted from God.

> To speak in brief, God is ineffable to his Son. For he is to himself what he is, that is, unspeakable. So that nothing which is called comprehensible does the Son know how to think about; for it is impossible for him to investigate the

74

Father, who is by himself. For the Son does not know his own essence: for, being Son, he really existed at the will of the Father. (*Ibid.*, p. 351.)

From these quotes, it is obvious that for Arius there was a great metaphysical gulf between God, the Father, and his (uniquely created) Logos or Son. Even though divine titles may be given to the unique, creaturely Son, he has no intimate relation with God for the simple reason that, in the final analysis he is a creature.

It may be said that Arius, his teachers and his supporters, were reading the Scriptures and interpreting theology from a Greek or hellenistic point of view. In the common cosmology of their time, the supreme God was seen as wholly separate from all created and material existence. Since Godhead is absolutely unique, wholly transcendent and totally indivisible by nature, its essence cannot be shared or communicated. The fact of the matter is that God is God and God is inescapably One! This position is not negotiable!

So the Son must be a creature, formed out of nothing by God, who in forming him becomes his "Father." As a creature, the Son had of necessity a beginning, even though this beginning is before the beginning of the universe and the angels. Further, being a creature, the Son has no direct, genuine knowledge of the Father, since he belongs to an entirely different plane of existence and is of a wholly different essence. So the Father remains ineffable to his Son, who, being a creature, is by definition liable to change and error (for only the true God is unchangeable). Nevertheless, the Arians did allow that the Son as creature could be called by divine names, but these were only courtesy titles. However, they searched the Scriptures of the Old and New Testaments to come up with texts which suggested that the Son was a creature and that, as such, he was subject to ignorance, weakness, suffering and personal development.

The late Dr. Philip E. Hughes, an Anglican clergyman, gave a very good summary of the nature of Arianism as a theological system when he wrote:

> The Christ devised by Arius was in being as remote from man as he was from God. Sharing neither in man's time nor in God's eternity, he was supposed to serve as a buffer to keep God and matter from direct contact with each other; but then he had to be defined as himself the first creature, before whose begetting God was not the Father, and whose own creation was willed in order that he might become the agent of the creation of all things else. To postulate that he was brought into being nontemporally or pretemporally in no way saved him from being bounded by temporality. The assertion that "there was once when he was not," even though the word "time" is not mentioned, is an inescapably temporal assertion. Estranged from the essential nature and the essential power of God, he cannot in any absolute sense be described as the Son of God and the Divine Word, but only in a reduced deferential sense as a concession to the uniqueness of his intermediate position. Arius' Christological statements define an ontology that is concerned with and controlled by questions of cosmology rather than soteriology: and it was soteriology that was ultimately at issue. (*The True Image*, p. 268.)

Put very simply, the Arian Christ could be neatly fitted into current hellenistic cosmology, but he could not be presented as the Savior of the world to whom the Gospels and Epistles witness! In Arianism, the Gospel is in the service of hellenistic metaphysics and cosmology. In orthodoxy, as we shall see, hellenistic techniques are in the service of the Gospel!

In the light of this exposition of the theological position of Arius, it is not surprising that the following anathemas containing its characteristic tenets were added to the Nicene Creed in 325 at the First Ecumenical Council.

> **Those who say that "There was once when he was not,"
> and "Before he was begotten he was not," and that "He
> was made of things that were not," or say that he is "of a
> different substance or essence," or that the Son is a crea-
> ture or changeable or transformable—these persons the
> holy, catholic and apostolic Church anathematizes.**

While Arianism was defeated at the Council, it was not immediately defeated within the Church throughout the Roman
Empire. Its appeal there, as indicated above, was its seeming
agreement with current and widely known hellenistic cosmology. Arianism was culturally acceptable while Orthodoxy was
not.

DEVELOPING FORMS OF ARIANISM

Arius and his supporters rejected the use of the word
homoousios ("consubstantial" or "of the same essence") to describe the relation of the Father and the Son. To them the Son
was *heteroousios*, "different in substance/essence." However,
some of the less radical were happy to use the similar (in terms
of spelling) but very different word (in terms of meaning),
homoiousios. The addition of the iota changes the meaning from
"of the same" to "of similar" *ousia* (essence), and thus, can
serve the aim of separating the Son metaphysically and
ontologically from the Father. So it is not surprising that the
opponents of the Nicene Faith—Arians and others—were ready
to speak of the Trinity as consisting of Three Persons (*treis
hypostaseis*), but not of Three equal Persons (as in classic orthodoxy) within one Godhead. In Arianism, the Three—the Father and the Son and the Holy Spirit—were three different beings, with only the Father being truly God and the other two
being unique creatures of this God in unique relations of order
to him (hence a holy Trinity).

Later, during the rule of Constantius from 350 to 361, the
Nicene Faith was openly attacked, and a radical form of

77

Arianism made its position known, whose advocates and supporters were known as the Anomoeans. They taught that the Son was unlike (*anomoios*) the Father. A statement of faith produced by a synod held at Sirmium in 357 explicitly forbad the use of either the *homoousios* or the *homoiousios* (which by this time was the word favored by the moderates who did not think of themselves as heretical Arians)! The content of this confession of belief led St. Hilary to describe the document as a blasphemy! Though a Trinity was confessed by the Arians it was a Trinity in which the Son is unlike the Father in essence; and the Spirit, though a creature like the Son, is also unlike the Son in essence and being. Here the Spirit is a "third power" and of "the third rank."

The opponents of the Nicene *homoousios* who favored *anomoios* went too far and efforts were made by some who took a middle ground to try to find a compromise. In this context, the word *homoios* (like in all respects) was suggested and approved by the Emperor. For all practical purposes the public faith of the Church soon became Homoean, a position which the Emperor believed allowed all reasonable churchmen to exist alongside each other in the one Church. This "neutral" faith (which effectively opened the door wide for all kinds of Arianism) was set forth in creeds produced by various synods in 359 and 360. As he pondered all this, St. Jerome wrote his now famous words—"the whole world groaned and was astonished to find itself Arian" (*Dialogue of a Luciferian and an Orthodox Christian*, p. 19). We may also recall that between the years 336 and 366 that most celebrated defender of the Nicene Faith, Athanasius, who had become Bishop of Alexandria in 328, was often assailed by wicked slanders of the Arians and endured five periods of banishment or exile from his diocese.

The most well known product of the Homoean position is the Creed produced at a synod in Constantinople in January

360. It is rather clumsy in style, but does exclude the Anomoeans:

We believe in one God, the Father almighty, from whom are all things;

We believe in the only begotten [unique] Son of God, who was begotten from God before all ages and before all beginning, through whom all things came into existence, both visible and invisible, begotten uniquely, alone from the Father alone, God from God, like [*homoios*] the Father who begot him, according to the Scriptures, whose generation no one knows save alone the Father who begot him. We know that this only-begotten [unique] Son of God came from heaven, the Father sending him, as it is written, for the destruction of sin and death, and was born of [the] Holy Spirit, of Mary the Virgin as regards the flesh, as it is written, and consorted [companied] with the disciples, and having fulfilled all the economy according to the Father's will, was crucified and died, and was buried and descended to the lower world (before whom hell itself trembled): who also rose again from the dead on the third day, and sojourned with the disciples, and when forty days were fulfilled was taken up to heaven, and sits on the Father's right hand, purposing to come on the last day, of the resurrection, in the Father's glory so as to render to each according to his deeds.

We believe in the Holy Spirit, whom the only-begotten [unique] Son of God himself, Christ our Lord and God, promised to send as a Paraclete to the race of men, as it is written, "The Spirit of truth," whom he sent to them when he had ascended into heaven.

But as for the word "substance" [*ousia*], which was used by the Fathers in simplicity, but, being unknown to the people caused scandal because the Scriptures themselves do not contain it, it has pleased us that it should be abolished and that no mention at all should be made of it in the future, since indeed the divine Scriptures nowhere have made mention of the substance of the Father and the Son. Nor indeed should the term "hypostasis" be used of the Father and the Son and the Holy Spirit.

But we say the Son is like the Father, as the divine Scriptures say and teach. But let all heresies which have either been condemned previously, or have come about more recently and are in opposition to this creed, be anathema.

This Creed became the official statement of what was to be (by the supporters of the Nicene *homoousios*) called Arianism in the period leading up to the Council of Constantinople in 381. However, as far as the Emperor was concerned the Creed was the Faith of the Church and he sent it to all Bishops requiring them to sign it.

Between 360 and 381, there was a drawing together in understanding of the Homoeousians (who favored the *homoiousios* and opposed both the Anomoeans and the Homoeans) and the Homoousians (who stood by the Nicene *homoousios*). By this time the debate also specifically included the status of the Holy Spirit in relation to the Father. Is the Holy Spirit "of like essence" or "of unlike essence" to, or just "like," the Father? Therefore, due to the convergence of aim and doctrine, it was possible at the Council of Constantinople in 381 for the 150 bishops both to confirm the Faith of Nicea, with its *homoousios* and its anathemas against original Arianism, and to promulgate a further Creed, which confirmed the faith of Nicea and also stated the full divinity of the Holy Spirit.

Further, the Fathers at the Council of Constantinople (381) declared the following in the first of their seven canons:

The profession of faith of the holy Fathers who gathered at Nicea in Bithynia is not to be abrogated, but is to remain in force. Every heresy is to be anathematized and

in particular that of the Eunomians or Anomoeans, that
of the Arians or Eudoxians, that of the Semi-Arians or
Pneumatochoi, that of the Sabellians, that of the
Marcellians, that of the Photinians and that of the
Apollinarians.

We must attempt to identify the groups which are anathematized.

The "Eunomians or Anomoeans" were the ultra Arians who
said that the Son and the Spirit are unlike the Father. Eunomius
was the Bishop of Cyzicus in Mysia, Asia Minor, and he was
very active in promoting the rejection of both the *homoousios*
and the *homoiousios*. He served the orthodox cause in the sense
that the Cappadocian Fathers (Basil the Great, Gregory of
Nazianzus and Gregory of Nyssa) shaped their doctrine of God
and human knowledge largely in response to what they perceived to be the errors of Eunomius.

The "Arians or Eudoxians" were the new Arians of the period from 360 onwards. They preferred the vague statement
that the Son and the Spirit are "like" (*homoios*) the Father.
Eudoxius was first Bishop of Antioch (358) and then Bishop of
Constantinople (360-370). He first favored the Anomoean position, but later embraced the Homoean theology.

The "Semi-Arians or Pneumatochoi [= Spirit-fighters]" referred to those who were opposed to the full divinity of the
Holy Spirit, but who counted in their number some who were
prepared to say of the Son that he was at least *homoiousios*
(and maybe even *homoousios*) with the Father. What they were
generally prepared to affirm of the Holy Spirit is that he is neither God nor a creature, but occupies some middle position.
They claimed that Scripture did not clearly state that the Holy
Spirit belonged wholly to the Godhead.

The "Sabellians" were named after Sabellius, of whom vir-
tually nothing is known. Sabellians sought to safeguard monotheism and at the same time be Trinitarian by claiming that the
Father, the Son and the Holy Spirit are three manifestations or

phases or showings of the One God (as if God were a Triangle with a name for each of the three sides). Thus, while the Unity of God was absolutely real, the Trinity of God was metaphysically unreal, for the Three were only an appearance and an accommodation to mankind. Other names for this heresy are Modalism or Modalistic Monarchianism. Naturally Sabellians could use *homoousios* of the Father, the Son and the Holy Spirit, but not in a Nicene sense! For them it meant that God is One indivisible Substance or Essence or Nature, whom Christians see as Three in One.

The "Marcellians" were named after Marcellus, Bishop of Ancyra, an extremist who strongly supported the *homoousios* but in what seemed to many to be a Sabellian direction. Apparently he taught that the Son and the Spirit only emerged within the Godhead for the purpose of creation and redemption. Thus when all the work of redemption is done they will be "reabsorbed" into the unity of the Godhead. The clause, "his kingdom will have no end," in the Creed of Constantinople (381) was inserted against this heresy.

The "Photinians" were the supporters of Photinus, Bishop of Sirmium and a disciple of Marcellus of Ancyra. He also taught a provocative form of Sabellianism.

The "Apollinarians" were the followers of Apollinarius, who was Bishop of Laodicea in the second part of the fourth century. Their heresy is strictly speaking a Christological heresy in contrast to a Trinitarian heresy for it relates to the make-up of the Person of Christ (the union within him of the divine and human natures). We shall examine its content in Part Three.

Finally, a word about the translation of *homoousios*. The traditional translation into English is either "consubstantial" or "of the same substance." Some favor "coessential" or "of the same being" because of the connotation widely attached to the term "substance" as descriptive of three-dimensioned solidity. We shall use any of these translations according to context, and to present a justifiable variety of expression.

FOR FURTHER READING

The two books by J. N. D. Kelly, *Early Christian Doctrines,* rev. ed. (San Francisco: Harper, 1978) and *Early Christian Creeds* (New York: Longman, 1991), are of great value. For translations from original documents see J. Stevenson, ed., *A New Eusebius: Documents Illustrative of the History of the Church to A.D. 337* (London: SPCK, 1957). The exposition of patristic Christology by Philip E. Hughes in his *The True Image: The Origin and Destiny of Man in Christ* (Grand Rapids: Eerdmans, 1989) is accurate and readable. Also valuable is R. P. C. Hanson, *The Search for the Christian Doctrine of God: The Arian Controversy, 318-381* (Edinburgh: T & T Clark, 1988).

CHAPTER SIX

Orthodoxy Proclaimed—
The Homoousios

Outside the inspired and authoritative content of the Holy Scriptures, there is probably not a more important word in the Christian vocabulary than the Greek word *homoousios* as it is found in both the Creed of Nicea (325) and the Creed of Constantinople (381). Another way of stating this is to say that the phrase, "Of one substance [essence] with the Father" (in Greek, *homoousion to patri*) as declaring the truth concerning Jesus Christ is crucial for the existence of Christianity. However, it is a phrase which must be clearly understood in terms of what it is stating both positively and negatively. The Creeds declare that there is one Godhead and that Godhead is wholly possessed not only by the Father, but also by the Son. Thus, in terms of Deity the Father and the Son, though distinct as Persons, are of one essence (or "of one substance" or "consubstantial"). And if the Father and the Son, though distinct, each possesses the whole Godhead entirely, then it cannot be said of the Son that his deity ("essence" or "substance") is like that of the Father.

THE CREED OF NICEA (325)

The confession of faith by the Bishops began with the expression of belief in the one true and living God, known in the Old Testament as *Yahweh Elohim* (the LORD God) and known in the New Testament as *ho Pater*, "the Father of our Lord Jesus Christ." It is important to note that the "one God" is not the Godhead but "the Father Almighty." This God, the Father, is the Creator of the whole universe, wherein man dwells, and of the whole invisible heaven, wherein the angels dwell.

In the second paragraph, the Bishops described and proclaimed the Lord Jesus Christ in whom they believed. Using titles and descriptions from Scripture, especially the Gospel of John, they called him the "Son of God" and "the only-begotten of the Father." Following the teaching of John 1, Colossians 1 and Hebrews 1, they proclaimed that the Father created the heavens and the earth through this same Jesus Christ. And following the Gospel accounts they spoke of the Incarnation of the Son, his manhood, his suffering, his death, his resurrection, his ascension and his future coming as the Judge. In all this they took for granted the pre-existence of the Son before his becoming man.

The big question they faced was not whether or not the Son was pre-existent. All agreed that the Son existed before he actually became man. The question was: "What is the relation of the Son to the Father?" In answer the Bishops at Nicea declared:

> **[the only-begotten Son is] from the substance of the Father, God from God, Light from Light, true God from true God, begotten not made, of one substance with the Father...**

The wording was intended to be anti-Arian and to make it very clear that the Son was not a creature.

That Jesus Christ is "from the very essence or substance (*ousia*) of the Father" was intended to clarify the previous words, **begotten from the Father.** Contrary to the Arian claim that the Son had been created out of nothing before the creation of the heavens and earth, the Bishops insisted that the Son is generated out of the Father's very essence, substance and being.

Jesus Christ is "true God from true God"—the Father Almighty is "true God" and Jesus Christ is also "true God" from the One who is the "true God." That is, Jesus is not called God as a title of honor as Arians maintained. He is truly God in whatever sense the Father is truly God.

Jesus Christ is "begotten not made." Arians used the verb "to beget" of the Son in relation to the Father, but by it they meant "to make." In contrast, the Son, as the tradition since Origen had taught, is eternally begotten of the Father.

Finally, Jesus Christ is "of one substance with the Father." Here is the use of *homoousios* and it is clearly intended to imply that the Son fully shared the deity, divinity and Godhead of the Father.

To make the rejection of Arianism as clear as possible, the bishops pronounced anathemas at the end of the Creed of 325 upon several typical phrases, catchwords and slogans written by Arius in his book of verse, *Thalia*. The statements condemned were:

> **There was when the Son was not.**
> **Before being born the Son was not.**
> **The Son came into existence out of nothing.**
> **The Son is of a different hypostasis or substance to the Father.**
> **The Son is created.**
> **The Son is subject to alteration or change.**

Thus the positive faith is that the Son is from the same eternity as is the Father, that he is of the same essential deity as is the Father and that he is immutable.

OUSIA & HOMOOUSIOS

In affirming that the Son is of the same, identical essence, substance and being as the Father by using the word *homoousios,* the Bishops moved outside Scriptural language. They would certainly have preferred to have used only Scriptural phrases and words in confessing the precise relation of the Son to the Father. However, when they tried to do so they found that the Arians had already given their own interpretation to those phrases. Thus, in order to state what they believed the sacred Scripture actually taught concerning Jesus Christ, they turned to the compound adjective, *homoousios*, with *ousia* as its principal element.

The word *ousia* had several meanings in Greek philosophical writings and the Bishops were obviously aware of these. So they were aware that in using the adjective, *homoousios*, as well as the noun, *ousia*, in the Creed, they were using words with several possible meanings—but they knew, and the Arians knew, that all the meanings were within the range of "substance" and "being" and "essence" and thus "identical substance" and "identical being" and "identical essence." Thus, in selecting this word for inclusion in the Creed, the Bishops intended it to make clear in as formal a way as possible that the truth of the Gospel is that the Son is truly God, in the sense that he fully shares the one, divine nature which his Father has.

In setting forth this teaching concerning the relation of the Son to the Father, the Bishops not only proclaimed the truth of the Gospel, they also produced the first statement of *dogma*—that the Son is of one substance with the Father. In short, the use of the *homoousios* is the first, official statement of the dogma of the Holy Trinity, even though the Nicene Creed of 325 expresses belief "in the Holy Spirit" in minimum words. At later Councils, the full dogma that both the Son and the Holy Spirit are of one substance with the Father and with each other will be set forth in detail. In fact, the general doctrine of the Trinity in the Nicene Creed is what has been called the doctrine of the economic Trinity—creation and salvation "from the Father through the Son and in the Spirit." But into this presentation of the economic Trinity there is placed a truth—the *homoousios*—which belongs to what is called the doctrine of the immanent or ontological Trinity (God-as-God-is-unto-himself).

The presentation of the Holy Trinity in the Bible is of God in action as the Creator, the Savior, and the Judge. The movement from God to man is "from the Father through the Son and in the Holy Spirit." Likewise the movement from man to God is "to the Father through the Son and in the Holy Spirit." In the use of the *homoousios* the Bishops were describing God as God is unto himself. They were speaking of the internal relation of the Father and the Son, and by implication of the Father and the Holy Spirit. In fact, the word "theology" developed the restricted meaning in the Church of the contemplation of the immanent or ontological Trinity, the true study of the Father, the Son and the Holy Spirit, one in *ousia*. (Later the distinction between the immanent and economic Trinity was put in terms of the contrast of the essence and the energies of God. However, the essence is known only through the energies of God and the immanent Trinity known only through the economic Trinity.)

Of course, there were dangers in using the word *homoousios*. One such danger was encouraging the development of Sabellianism and another was of being interpreted as Sabellian. Certainly some Arians, as well as others more kindly disposed to the Nicene Creed, believed that to use *homoousios* was actually to mean that God is a Unity and that in that Unity there cannot be any genuine plurality (Trinity). Thus, what Christians call the Holy Trinity would be a Trinity of appearance, not a Trinity of reality. For Sabellianism there are three Modes or Manifestations of the Unity, so that the one God is known successively (or even simultaneously) as the Father, the Son and the Spirit. In terms of salvation history, some Sabellians said that the Old Testament reveals God in the Mode of Father, the Gospels reveal God in the Mode of the Son, and the Acts and Epistles reveal God in the Mode of the Holy Spirit.

We may note in passing that Sabellianism was a continuing problem for the Church in the West and that the *Quicunque Vult* or the *Athanasian Creed* was composed and used to combat the doctrine that the Father, the Son and the Holy Spirit were simply Modes of the One God. (See further J. N. D. Kelly, *The Athanasian Creed*, 1965.)

Though some of the orthodox party of the fourth century did lean towards Sabellianism, the major supporters of the Nicene Creed always insisted that the Holy Trinity is a genuine Trinity of Persons. The Father is not the Son and the Son is not the Father even though, importantly, they share one and the same deity and divinity. Apart from having to make clear that they were not Sabellians, the orthodox also had to develop a vocabulary to speak of the Holy Trinity in such a way that what was being affirmed could not easily be misunderstood and misinterpreted.

WHY PRECISION IN DOCTRINE?

But why was precision of definition so necessary? Why did the orthodox fight so long and so hard to retain the *homoousios*? Why was a right doctrine of the relation of Jesus Christ to the Father so important? Several answers were given and may still be given to these questions.

First of all, the Bishops believed that God had acted and spoken in Jesus Christ and that the Church had the solemn and sacred duty of speaking rightly of Jesus Christ, his identity and his mission. If God had provided a revelation of who he is and who is his Son, then the Church must surely study and set forth that truth.

In the second place, they judged that Arianism, when fully seen for what it was, was nothing more than a form of polytheism. Instead of the Holy Triad/Trinity, the Arians were worshipping three deities related to one another in a hierarchy—a form of tritheism. Certainly one (God the Father) was absolutely supreme, but the other two (the Son and the Spirit) were certainly not either angels or men and so were inferior deities.

Thirdly, the Bishops knew that Arianism undermined their whole tradition of worship and prayer. Not only did they baptize converts in the one name of the Father and the Son and the Holy Spirit, they also addressed prayers both to the Father and to the Son. They worshipped God in and through God—the Father through the Son and in the Holy Spirit.

In the fourth place, the Bishops, Athanasius in particular, knew that Arianism proposed a Mediator, who could not truly be a Savior. A created being, however wonderfully created and gloriously endowed, could not save a people from sin, death and Satan. He could teach them, perform miracles and provide an example to them, but he could not save them from eternal death into eternal life. Only a Savior who is truly God become man can restore sinful, diseased man to a right relation and communion with the Father. That is, only a Savior who is *homoousios* with the Father can be the Savior of the world.

Finally, as we noted in the last chapter, the Bishops judged that Arianism was primarily a form of Greek cosmology. It used the Christian biblical data to fill out in a religious sense the commonly held Greek view of God (gods) and the cosmos. Thus, it was a sell-out to a sophisticated form of paganism.

THE CREED OF CONSTANTINOPLE (381)

We have already noted that the Creed of 381 is not identical with that of 325. In fact, it is a related but different Creed, which retains the *homoousios* concerning the Son and declares the true deity of the Holy Spirit.

The first part of the second paragraph of the Creed of 381 sets forth the relation of Jesus Christ to the Father in these words:

We believe in one Lord Jesus Christ, the only begotten Son of God, begotten from the Father before all ages, light from light, true God from true God, begotten not made, of one substance [*homoousios*] with the Father, through whom all things came into existence, who because of us men and because of our salvation came down from heaven, and was incarnate from the Holy Spirit and the Virgin Mary and became man....

This is somewhat less emphatic than is the similar paragraph in the Nicene Creed. One reason for this is that the Nicene Creed is taken for granted as being in existence and as being received as the Faith by the Church.

Here, in the context of proclaiming the economic Trinity (creation and redemption from the Father through the Son by the Holy Spirit), the Bishops proclaim the reality of the immanent Trinity. They confess the truth concerning the Son of God— the truth to which the Scriptures point and bear witness. Thus, as with the Nicene Creed, they make clear that the relation of the Son to the Father is not that of being created or physically procreated before or with space and time. Rather, the relation is that of the Son always possessing the very essence or substance or deity of the Father without being the Father. The Son is "true God of true God." Always and forever ("before all ages") the Father shares his deity with his Son so that the Son always has exactly the one and the same deity as does the Father. The Son is "of one substance with the Father." Yet the Son, is not the Father, and the Father is not the Son. And, it is the Son not the Father who is incarnate from the Holy Spirit and the Virgin Mary.

The words "was incarnate from the Holy Spirit and the Virgin Mary" serve to make clear the fact that there was a real and true incarnation of the eternal Word. As the incarnate Son, and known as Jesus of Nazareth, the eternal Word loved, trusted and obeyed the Father and did all that he did in his manhood through the inspiration, illumination and power of the Holy Spirit. So he was confessed as the Messiah, the Christ, the Lord. It is this Story which the Four Gospels tell and the Epistles interpret. It is the Story of the "oikonomia" (the ordered process of the self-disclosure of God), the action of God as the economic Trinity. Yet in and through the economic Trinity is necessarily seen by the eyes of faith the immanent Trinity; and (as the Bishops so clearly recognized) the only way to safeguard the economic Trinity and ensure the confession that the Son of God is truly and really the genuine Savior of the world is to speak truthfully of the immanent Trinity. Thus, the inescapability of the confession that the Son is *homoousios* with the Father (and with the Holy Spirit).

By the time of the Council of Constantinople, there was a general agreement among the orthodox concerning the vocabulary to be used to speak of the Holy Trinity—i.e., one *ousia* in three *hypostaseis*; three Persons in and of one Substance or Essence. There had been a clarifying of the doctrine of the Holy Spirit initially by Athanasius (see especially his *Letters to Serapion,* who was the Bishop of Thmuis in the Nile delta in Egypt) and then by the Cappadocian Fathers, Basil and the two Gregorys. Between 370 and the Council of Constantinople in 381, the latter brought clarity of expression to the doctrines concerning both the Person of the Holy Spirit and the nature of the Holy Trinity .

Basil composed *De Spiritu sancto* (375) in which he argued that the Holy Spirit is to be given the same glory, honor and worship as are the Father and the Son, for he is not below them but with them in the Unity of the Godhead. Also in this treatise, he discussed the various possible renderings of the doxology ("glory to the Father through the Son in the Holy Spirit," and "glory be to the Father with the Son and with the Holy Spirit") claiming that both were orthodox. However, as a result of the desire to avoid possible Arian teaching, what we now know as the *Gloria* (the second of those cited) won out in the liturgy of the Church. Thus, today in the West we say, "Glory be to the Father and to the Son and to the Holy Spirit: as it was in the beginning, is now and ever shall be, world without end. Amen."

Gregory of Nazianzus proclaimed even more clearly than did Basil the divinity of the Holy Spirit and the truth that the Spirit is *homoousios* with the Father and the Son. However, he was very conscious of the late development in the Church of a clear sense of the full divinity of the Holy Spirit and he offered this brief explanation. "The Old Testament announces the Father clearly and the Son obscurely. The New Testament has manifested the Son, but it has only indicated the divinity of the Holy Spirit. At present, the Spirit is among us and shows himself in all his splendor. It would not have been prudent, before one recognized the divinity of the Father, to preach openly the divinity of the Son, and as long as that of the Son was not accepted, to impose the Holy Spirit—if I may dare to express myself thus" (*Oration* 31.26).

Both Gregory of Nazianzus and Gregory of Nyssa were active in the Council of Constantinople (381). The third paragraph of the Creed approved there, is much longer than that of the Nicene Creed and reads:

We believe in the Holy Spirit, the Lord and life-giver, who proceeds from the Father, who with the Father and the Son is together worshipped and together glorified, who spoke through the prophets...

There is no claim here that the Holy Spirit is actually one in substance with the Father and the Son. The word *homoousios* is avoided in order to gain the acceptance of the Creed by all present in the Council. However, what is said of the Holy Spirit is clearly sufficient to make clear that he possesses true divinity and is really God.

To call the Holy Spirit "Lord" is to follow St. Paul (II Cor. 3:17ff.); to call him the "life-giver" is to follow St. John and St. Paul (John 6:63 and II Cor. 3:6). The description of the Spirit proceeding from the Father is based on the words of Jesus recorded in John 15:26 (see also St. Paul in I Cor. 2:12). And the claim that the Spirit spoke through the prophets is based on St. Peter in II Peter 1:21.

However, it is in the words "who with the Father and the Son is together worshipped and together glorified" that the Council set forth most clearly its belief in the divinity of the Holy Spirit. These words were taken from St. Basil's treatise on the Holy Spirit, to which we made reference above. To say that the Church is to worship and to give glory to the Father with the Son and with the Holy Spirit is to say in the language of worship what the *homoousios* states in the language of dogma. This fact was recognized by the Second Council of Constantinople (554) which confirmed that the confession of orthodoxy is: "We believe there is one substance (*ousia*) of the Father and the Son and the Holy Spirit in three most perfect Subsistences or Persons ."

Worship (adoration) and glory are what the Church offers in its praise to the Three Persons (not specifically to the Godhead which they share). The expression "together with" emphasizes that the Three who are "co-adored" are distinct from each other, but that the motive of their adoration is one and the same. Therefore, one can adore the Father alone, but one cannot adore the Father exclusively for he is truly the Father of the Son and the Father from whom proceeds the Holy Spirit. To adore the one Person is by necessity to adore all Three, because there is one substance of the Father and the Son and the Holy Spirit.

Regrettably no copy of the Ecumenical Council's doctrinal decisions known as "The Tome" has survived. However, there is a summary of its doctrine in the Synodical Letter produced by the local synod of Constantinople in 382, the year after the Ecumenical Council in the same city. It will be helpful to quote from it where it expounds the orthodox teaching on the Holy Trinity with reference to the received Faith:

> **This Faith...is the most ancient, and accords with the creed of our Baptism, and teaches us to believe in the name of the Father and of the Son and of the Holy Spirit: believing, that is to say, that the Father and the Son and the Holy Spirit have a single Godhead and power and substance, a dignity deserving the same honor and a co-eternal sovereignty, in three most perfect Hypostases [subsistences], or three perfect Persons. So there is no place for Sabellius' diseased theory in which the Hypostases are confused and thus their proper characteristics destroyed. Nor may the blasphemy of Eunomians and Arians and Pneumatomachi prevail, with its division of substance or nature or of Godhead, and its introduction of some nature which was produced subsequently, or was created, or was of a different substance, into the uncreated and consubstantial and co-eternal Trinity.**

Thus by 381, the full dogma of the consubstantial Holy Trinity had been created and received by the Church. From now on anything that fell short of this dogma, or exceeds it, or is contrary to it, would be judged as erroneous and heretical. (For the addition of the *Filioque* to the Creed in the West see Appendix I, "I believe/We believe.")

When the doctrine of the Trinity finally came to be formulated as one *ousia* in three *hypostaseis*, this implied the following. God, from the point of view of internal analysis, is one object; but, from the point of view of external presentation, God is three objects. His unity is safeguarded by the teaching that these three objects of presentation (*hypostaseis*) are not merely precisely similar (as the Semi Arians admitted), but in a true sense, identically one. So the sum God+God+God is not three Gods, but is simply God! This is "because the word God, as applied to each Person of the Trinity distinctly, expresses a

Totum and Absolute which is incapable of increment either in quantity or in quality" (Prestige, *God*, p. 169).

FOR FURTHER READING

G. L. Prestige, *God in Patristic Thought* (London: William Heinemann, 1936), is still excellent reading, as is also Vladimir Lossky, *The Mystical Theology of the Eastern Church* (London: James Clarke, 1957). The writings of Athanasius and the Cappadocian fathers, Basil and the two Gregorys, may be read in English in the appropriate volumes of the series *A Select Library of Nicene and Post-Nicene Fathers of the Christian Church* (New York: Christian Literature Company, 1890-1900; reprint, Peabody, MA: Hendrickson Publishers, Inc., 1994). Of great value also is the selection of documents in J. Stevenson, ed., *Creeds, Councils and Controversies*: *Documents Illustrative of the History of the Church, A.D. 337-461* (London: SPCK, 1966). Some of the writings of the two Gregorys are in Edward R. Hardy, *Christology of the Later Fathers* (Philadelphia: Westminster Press, 1966). For a detailed study of *ousia* see G. C. Stead, *Divine Substance* (Oxford: Clarendon Press, 1977).

PART THREE:

THE LORD JESUS CHRIST

It is necessary for salvation to believe faithfully the incarnation of our Lord Jesus Christ. The right faith, therefore, is that we believe and confess that our Lord Jesus Christ, the Son of God, is God and man. God, of the substance of the Father, begotten before the ages; and man, of the substance of his mother, born in the world. Perfect God, perfect man, subsisting of a rational soul and human flesh. Equal to the Father according to his Godhead, less than the Father according to his humanity. Although he is God and man, he is not two, but one Christ. One, however, not by conversion of the Godhead into flesh, but by the taking of humanity into God. One altogether, not by confusion of substance, but by unity of Person. For as a reasoning soul and flesh is one man, so God and man is one Christ.

Quicunque Vult or The Athanasian Creed

CHAPTER SEVEN

The Son of God Incarnate

At Caesarea Philippi, the apostles were required by Jesus to state who he was. Peter, their spokesman, illuminated of mind by the Father in heaven through the divine Spirit, cried out: "Thou art the Christ, the Son of the living God!" (Matt.16:13-20). Some eighteen months before this event, and at the very beginning of his ministry, Jesus was baptized by John and immediately afterwards "the heavens were opened and Jesus saw the Spirit of God descending like a dove, and alighting on him; and lo, a voice from heaven, saying, 'This is my beloved Son, with whom I am well pleased'" (Matt. 3:16-17). The Father's voice was heard once again from heaven—a week or so after Peter's confession at Caesarea Philippi—in the amazing event we call the Transfiguration of Jesus. From within the cloud, the symbol of the holy presence of Yahweh, came the words to be heard by Moses, Elijah and the three apostles, "This is my beloved Son, with whom I am well pleased; listen to him." As they heard the words they saw Jesus: "his face shone like the sun, and his garments were white as light" (Matt. 17:1-8).

The apostles had no doubt that Jesus was a man because they lived with him daily and saw him being and doing all the things which a man normally does. The apostles also had no doubt that Jesus was more than a mere man: he was the Son of God who enjoyed a unique relation to Yahweh, whom he called "my Father."

SETTING THE CONTEXT

To appreciate why and how the early Church arrived at its official teaching or dogma concerning Jesus Christ as One Person made known in two natures, we need to remember that the discussions and resolutions followed the acceptance of the doctrine of the Holy Trinity of the Creeds of Nicea (325) and Constantinople (381). So in theological controversy and dialogue, it was taken for granted from the fourth to the seventh century that Jesus Christ was in a unique relation to God the Father, and that he was pre-existent before his birth from holy Mary the Virgin. In fact, he was the Son of the Father, Only-begotten, and of the same, identical Godhead as the Father. Therefore, in patristic teaching the fact that the coeternal and consubstantial Son of God should become a first-century Jewish man is not primarily a *problem* for Christology; it is its *presupposition.*

Thus, the major questions concerning his identity and role assumed that he was truly divine. He was God the Word made flesh, and he was the Son of God become Man. The questions concerned (a) the reality of his flesh and manhood (Was he fully and truly a human being?), and (b) how he could be truly God (which the Creeds of 325 and 381 said he was) and truly Man (as the same Creeds also said he was) at the one and the same time, without being some kind of fusion of a heavenly Person and an earthly person?

In this specific context and to prepare my reader to appreciate the debates and the dogma of the early Church concerning Christology, I shall present evidence from the New Testament, which clearly assumes and/or points to the genuine humanity, real manhood and particularity of Jesus of Nazareth as a single, Jewish man. To recognize Jesus as a real man is hardly a problem for modern people, for they tend to begin their thinking concerning Christ the opposite way to that of the Fathers. Today theologians ask, "How can this Jewish Man be the eternal Son of God?" A long time ago the Fathers asked, "How can the eternal and Only-begotten Son of God be a genuine Man?" The changed questions reflects a changed cultural and religious environment. We live after the Enlightenment, and thus, tend to begin from human experience of the world, rather than the revealed knowledge from God.

WHAT IS MAN?

Before we can say whether or not Jesus was truly Man, we need to have some idea as to what a man is. Obviously, biologically speaking, he is a part of the animal creation. Yet, at the same time, he is different from the animals with whom he shares the earth. Man is not only a walking, talking and erect body in which are the physical organs such as a brain, liver and heart. He is a unity of mind (or soul) and body. He is a being who consciously knows what it is to think, to feel and to decide. He has not merely an animal soul, the center of his physical life, but a rational soul whereby he is able to enjoy communion with God and his fellow human beings and to contemplate the revelation of God given to him through the created order. He is like the animals in many respects, but in one major area he is different from them—he has a rational soul. Thus, man's true identity is more than the sum total of his bodily parts and their energies.

Who man is can only be stated when his inner self, his real being, his mind and his soul are taken into account along with, and in union with, his flesh and blood. He is a relational being whose spirit is able to commune with God, man and the created order in and through his bodily existence. He has reason, intelligence and imagination; he experiences and knows deep feelings/emotions/passions/affections, and he has freedom to make moral choices and decisions. However, his existence is filled with seeming paradoxes and conflicts, for he is not always what he intends to be or knows that he ought to be. His freedom is impaired, his soul diseased and his body subject to weakness, illness and death. He thinks, feels, says and does things in his bodily existence of which he is both pleased and ashamed. He is conscious of being alienated both from God and from his fellow men.

In the Old Testament, the word *basar* is usually translated as "flesh." Though it can mean the flesh of the animal that the butcher supplies as meat, it often means the whole body as flesh and blood and human nature (Prov. 14:30; Ps. 16:9). The union of two living beings, a man and his wife, is "one flesh" (Gen. 2:24). A man can say of his relatives, "I am your bone and your flesh" (Judg. 9:2). Thus, "all flesh" means the human race, and "What can flesh do to me?" (Ps. 56:4) means "What can mankind do to me?"

The Greek word *sarx* covers the same range of meanings as *basar*. Flesh can be meat (Rev. 19:18), the whole body (Gal. 4:13ff.) or the whole man (II Cor. 7:5). St. Paul spoke of Christ being descended from David "according to the flesh" as well as "Israel according to the flesh" (Rom. 1:3; 9:3; I Cor. 10:18). When it is affirmed that Christ has been "in the flesh" (see Eph. 2:15; I Pet. 3:18; I John 4:2), flesh means a full, physical existence.

Yet human beings are impaired and diseased by sin, and thus often flesh is not merely physical existence, it is man in his rebellion against God. In this context of thought, to set the mind on the flesh is to set the mind against God (Rom. 8:5-7). The flesh, being the union of body and human nature, is a center of opposition to the will of God. A dreadful list of the "works of the flesh" is provided by Paul in Galatians 5:19-21.

THE LOGOS BECAME FLESH

In his Prologue to the Gospel, John declared that "the Word (*Logos*) became flesh (*sarx*) and dwelt among us" (1:14). In the Epistles of John we read: "Every spirit which confesses that Jesus Christ is come in the flesh is of God" (I John 4:2) and "Many deceivers have gone out into the world, men who will not acknowledge the coming of Jesus Christ in the flesh" (II John 7).

In the Prologue, John did not write "became man" or "took a body" but "became flesh." The verb is in the aorist tense, indicating action at a point of time. "Flesh" is an emphatic way, perhaps even a crude way in this context, of emphasizing the reality of the human nature which the Word assumed. As he was probably facing some form of Docetism, in which Jesus Christ was said to look like and appear to be a man but not to have soiled himself with fleshly, bodily, physical human nature, John wrote "became flesh."

In the second part of verse 14, John uses more dignified language recalling Yahweh's glorious presence in the Tabernacle (Ezek. 37:27; Ex. 40:34ff.). Through the brief statement, "dwelt among us," and alluding to the Temple, he makes clear that God himself was present within the physical, human life of the Lord Jesus Christ.

But what kind of flesh is the flesh of the Logos, the Son of the Father, in his incarnate manhood? Is it the human nature which we all share which suffers from the disease of sin? Or is it the human nature of the first Adam, made in the image and after the likeness of God, and without sin? Paul taught that Jesus Christ is the New and the Second Adam (Rom. 5:12-21; I Cor. 15:45-47), whose human nature is without the stain and guilt of sin (II Cor. 5:21). In agreement, Peter declared that Christ "committed no sin; no guile was found on his lips" (I Pet. 2:22). Therefore, while Jesus is truly a man with a full human nature, he differs from fellow human beings in that he has no sin and did not sin.

The fact that Jesus Christ is without sin does not mean that he cannot fully identify with, and be the representative of, sinful humanity. His full identification with the reality of the human condition in order to be their Savior is emphasized in the Letter to the Hebrews where we read: "He had to be made like his brethren in every respect, so that he might become a merciful and faithful high priest in the service of God, to make expiation for the sins of his people" (2:17), and, "For we have not a high priest who is unable to sympathize with our weaknesses, but one who in every respect has been tempted as we are, yet without sinning" (4:15), and "Looking to Jesus the pioneer and perfecter of our faith, who for the joy that was set before him endured the cross, despising the shame" (12:2).

Paul also speaks of Jesus Christ in terms of a theology of representation. "For you know the grace of our Lord Jesus Christ, that though he was rich, yet for our sake he became poor, so that by his poverty you might become rich" (II Cor. 8:9); and "Though he was in the form of God, he did not count equality with God a thing to be grasped, but emptied himself, taking the form of a servant, being born in the likeness of men" (Phil. 2:6-7); and "For our sake he made him to be sin who knew no sin, so that in him we might become the righteousness of God" (II Cor. 5:21).

As the Word become flesh, and as the eternal Son of God, born of a woman in the fullness of time and under the Jewish Law (Gal. 4:4), Jesus Christ had truly come "in the flesh." For those with a Jewish background, to understand flesh as the fullness of human nature (body with soul) was relatively straightforward and unproblematic. In contrast, for those in Greek culture, where a clear distinction was usually made between the flesh (= physical body only) and the soul or mind, it was easy to assume that the Logos took actual flesh, but not a rational soul, in Mary's womb. Some of the Fathers produced imbalanced or erroneous Christologies because they took flesh in its hellenistic rather than its biblical meaning.

JESUS, THE MAN

A careful reading of the four Gospels will disclose that Jesus Christ (whatever else he was) was a real male human being. He was born of a human mother; he grew up as other boys did; he walked and he talked; he ate and he slept; he knew hunger, thirst, weariness, joy, sorrow, anger, God-forsakeness (on the Cross) and death.

Jesus was a first-century Palestinian Jew, sharing the physical and mental features of Jewish culture. Furthermore, he had a penis and was circumcised; he spoke Aramaic (and maybe also Hebrew and Greek); he taught as a traveling rabbi, interpreting his people's Scriptures; and he kept the Jewish festivals, engaged in prayer and offered sacrifice in the Temple.

Though the writers of the New Testament never explicitly state that Jesus as Man had a human mind-soul, they may be said to assume he did because they ascribe to him such mental acts and attitudes as joy and sorrow, compassion and anger, love and affection. The fact is that the four Evangelists have little or no interest in what we would call today the psychology of Jesus of Nazareth, but they do assume, and then proceed on the assumption, that Jesus is a real Man. Certainly, he is a unique Man and certainly he has a unique relation to Yahweh, the God of Israel. Nevertheless, the Evangelists portray him as truly, really and vitally as a Man among men. No person he ever met appears to have questioned whether he was truly a man—a male human being, not an angel or an embodied spirit!

Since he was a real man, Jesus must have passed through all the normal developmental stages of mind and body. The late Dr. Eric Mascall explained:

> Since human nature, in any individual, is not given from its beginning in a fully developed state but develops from the unrealized potentialities of the original fertilized ovum through birth, infancy, childhood, and adolescence to its cli-

max in adult manhood, we must surely hold that the mentality of Jesus, like that of any other human being, developed *pari passu* with the development of the bodily organism. To say this is not to imply that it was defective in the early stages; on the contrary, at each stage it was precisely what at that stage it is proper for human nature to be. It is surely a valid insight that asserts that you must not try to put an old head on young shoulders. It is not simply a discovery of modern anthropology that mental and physical (especially cerebral) functioning are intimately and intricately allied; it is inherent in the traditional Christian belief that a human being is not a pure spirit temporarily encapsulated in a body but is a bipartite psychological unity...A modern discussion of Jesus' human knowledge will need to take account of all that is now known about the psychophysical structure of the cognitive process and about the development of human mentality from its beginning in the fertilized ovum to its culmination in adulthood.

After noting that our modern scientific theories are always open to revision Dr. Mascall continued:

While Jesus' human nature is more and not less genuinely human for its assumption by the Person of the eternal Son of God [as set forth by the Council of Chalcedon], it may for that very reason be expected to manifest powers and capacities which outstrip those of human nature as we normally experience it in ourselves and in others. Some of these powers and capacities may pertain to Jesus simply because his human nature is unfallen and perfect, whereas ours is fallen and maimed, and, though redeemed, is still in process of recreation and restoration. Others may pertain to it because its Person is the divine Word, because "in him the whole fullness of deity dwells bodily" (Col.1:19). It may be difficult to discriminate in any given case between these alternatives; nor, I think, will it greatly matter, provided we keep a firm grasp upon the principle that, even in the supreme example of the Incarnation, grace does not suppress nature but perfects it. (*Whatever Happened to the Human Mind?* (London: SPCK, 1980), p. 45.)

Jesus of Nazareth was certainly more than, but he certainly was not less than, a full-blooded, fully human, and psychologically mature Man—"of a rational soul and body."

Perhaps the most obvious way to appreciate the true and full humanity and manhood of Jesus as it is presented in the New Testament is to pay attention to the theme of the obedience of Jesus to the will of God. Here we see the sinless humanity of Jesus in communion with the Father ever seeking to obey and please the Father, thereby acting as a true Adam and as a true incarnate Son. Yet this obedience was not that of an automaton, programmed to do the will of heaven. As the Letter to the Hebrews puts it: "Although he was a Son, he learned obedience through what he suffered and being made perfect he became the eternal source of salvation to all who obey him" (5:8-9). Paul speaks of Jesus Christ as the Suffering Servant who became "obedient unto death" (Phil. 2:8) and emphasizes that it is the free obedience of the New and Second Adam, Jesus Christ, which is the cause of human salvation—"As by one man's disobedience many were made sinners, so by one man's obedience many will be made righteous" (Rom. 5:19).

The reality and content of this obedience of Jesus to the Father's will is portrayed in the Gospels. As a twelve year old boy, Luke tells us that Jesus said to Mary and Joseph when they found him in the Temple, "Did you not know that I *must be* in my Father's house?" (2:47). Then, according to the same Gospel, the last words of Jesus as he died on the Cross were, "Father, into thy hands I commit my spirit" (23:46). Not long before these last words from Calvary's cross, Jesus had prayed in the Garden of Gethsemane, "Father, if thou art willing, remove this cup from me; nevertheless, not my will, but thine, be done" (22:42). And some months before his arrest, trial and crucifixion, knowing that the Father's will was for him to be the Suffering Servant of Isaiah's prophecies (52:13-53:12), Luke tells us that "when the days drew near for him to be received up, he set his face to go to Jerusalem" (9:51). Jesus knew what he was to face in Jerusalem because at his Transfiguration, Luke informs us, Moses and Elijah "appeared in glory and spoke of his Exodus which he was to accomplish at Jerusalem" (9:31). What the Father planned for the Incarnate Son was that he accomplish a new Exodus, the deliverance of his people from their sin, by his sacrificial, propitiatory and expiatory death at Calvary. Jesus freely and readily took upon himself this unique vocation even though at times he strained his human capacities to their limit.

The inner reality of this obedience of the Incarnate Son to the invisible Father is conveyed most powerfully and movingly by the Gospel of John. Jesus lives for the Father and to do the Father's bidding. His food is to do the will of the Father and finish the work that the Father gives him to do. The will of Jesus is wholly and lovingly willing to do what the Father wills. The Son is subordinate to the Father in that he does the will of the Father, because he loves the Father and is in continual communion with him. In will, in love, in knowledge, the Father and the incarnate Son are one. Thus, the last words of Jesus on the Cross were "It is finished" (John 19:30). The Father has been glorified by the Son, who has completed the work that He gave him to do.

Reflecting upon the statements in the Gospels and Epistles concerning the obedience of Jesus to his Father, we quickly come to the conclusion that Jesus was endowed with reason and free will. In other words, he possessed a mind-soul. Only a person with a full humanity can offer a voluntary obedience to God. In the case of Jesus Christ the obedience and self-sacrifice is not merely that of a great prophet and godly man. It is the self-sacrifice of the Word made flesh, the incarnate Son of the Father, and therefore it has a unique quality and efficacy— by his sacrifice he becomes the personal Mediator of salvation. And this salvation is of God, from the Father through the Son and in the Holy Spirit, as we noted in chapter four above.

The late Dr. Austin Farrer, Warden of Keble College, Oxford, reflected long on the Christian doctrine of the Incarnation of God and wrote:

> We cannot understand Jesus as simply the God-who-was-man. We have left out an essential factor, the sonship. Jesus is not simply God manifest as man: he is the divine Son coming in manhood. What was expressed in human terms here below was not bare deity; it was divine sonship. God cannot live an identically godlike life in eternity and in a human story. But the divine Son can make an identical response to the Father, whether in the love of the blessed Trinity or in the fulfillment of an earthly ministry. All the conditions of actions are different on the two levels: the filial response is one. Above, the appropriate response is a co-operation in sovereignty and an interchange of eternal joys. Then the Son gives back to the Father all that the Father is. Below, in the incarnate life, the appropriate response is an obedience to inspiration, a waiting for direction, an acceptance of suffering, a rectitude of choice, a resistance to temptation, a willingness to die. For such things are the stuff of our existence; and it was in this very stuff that Christ worked out the theme of heavenly sonship, proving himself on earth the very thing he was in heaven; that is, a continual act of filial love. (*The Brink of Mystery* (London: SPCK, 1976), p. 20.)

Thus it is that, while the filial response is one in heaven and on earth, "Our Lord Jesus Christ, the Son of God...is equal to the Father in respect of his divinity and less than the Father in respect to his humanity" (Athanasian Creed).

CONCERNING MARY

In today's generally liberal climate of thought, we find it easy and perhaps normal to speak of the humanity and manhood of Jesus, with only the briefest of references to his mother, Mary.

The accounts in the Gospels of Matthew and Luke make clear that in her conception of the fetus, Jesus, Mary did not have any sexual intercourse with a man, not even her betrothed, Joseph. What the sperm of man normally supplies was given from the Father through the Son and by the Holy Spirit, who overshadowed Mary at her conception. However, everything else as far as we know concerning her pregnancy and her giving birth to her Son, whom she called Jesus (= Joshua, "the LORD our salvation") was "normal," taking approximately nine months.

Therefore, it is clear that the human nature and flesh, or the body and soul, of Jesus came from his mother. But his actual sex as a male came from elsewhere! Obviously, Jesus was a male baby with all the physical organs and mental life which is part of maleness in the human species. This means, in terms of modern knowledge of chromosomes, that Jesus had chromosomes which included the Y chromosome, for it was this which made him male and not female. At the genetic level, females consist of identical genes (XX) and males of diverse ones (XY). Further, it means that the Holy Spirit supplied this Y chromosome because Mary, as a woman, only produced X type chromosomes. (In normal human reproduction the male alone is the arbiter of an offspring's sex.)

In early Christianity, the fact that Jesus had a real, biological, human mother was of great importance in teaching that Jesus was truly and really a male human being. Furthermore, the fact that Mary wholly cooperated with the will of God and said, "Be it unto me according to thy word," provided the Church with an example, a model, of what the Church as the Bride of Christ is to be—loving and obedient. As we shall see in chapter nine, the Church was to call her *Theotokos* not because she was God, but because she was, in a literal sense, the "God-bearer" or "the birth-giver of God;" her Son was the Word become flesh (her flesh!).

To quote Dr. Mascall again:

> It was male human *nature* that the Son of God united to his divine person; it was a female human *person* who was chosen to be his mother. In no woman has human *nature* been raised to the dignity which it possesses in Jesus of Nazareth, but to no male human *person* has there been given a dignity comparable to that which Mary enjoys as *Theotokos*, a dignity which, in the words of the Eastern liturgy, makes her "more honorable than the cherubim and beyond comparison more glorious than the seraphim." In Mary a woman became the mother of God, but to no man, not even to Joseph, was it given to be the father of God: that status belongs only to the Father in heaven. The centrality of womanhood in redemption is shown by the fact that the incarnation itself waited for the courageous and obedient *Fiat* of Mary (Luke 1:38); the initial reaction of the man, Joseph, however great his contribution later on, was to be doubtful about his fiancee's chastity (Matt. 1:18ff.). ("Some Basic Considerations" in Peter Moore, ed., *Man, Woman and the Priesthood* (London: SPCK), pp. 23-24.)

In the early Church, the way one viewed and spoke of Mary was a very clear indication of how one viewed and spoke of her Son.

FOR FURTHER READING

There are many books produced by modern biblical scholars, which attempt to present the Christology of the New Testament—e.g., by Oscar Cullman, Marin Hengel, C. H. Dodd, Howard Marshall, C. F. D. Moule, Raymond Brown and Joachim Jeremias. Yet, to appreciate the search of the Fathers for the truth concerning the Manhood of the Son and Word of God, one needs most of all to be familiar with the actual content of the Gospels and if possible with the claims of the Apostles in the Acts and the Letters.

CHAPTER EIGHT

Apollinarianism, Nestorianism and Monophysitism Rejected

If the Arian teaching had not been condemned because it failed to state truthfully the relation of Jesus Christ to the Father, it would have been condemned because it failed to confess the real and vital humanity of Jesus Christ. The Arians taught that Jesus did not have a human rational soul (a mind) because there was no need for one; his mind was that of the Word who took flesh to himself. In such teaching the Arians sounded like some of their opponents, who differed from them radically in the evaluation of the Word who took human flesh, but who actually believed with them that Jesus Christ had no human mind. As we have seen, for the Arians the Word was a created being; for their opponents the Word was uncreated and *homoousios* with the Father.

In this chapter, it is our task to look at the major forms of Christological heresy which came on the scene in the fourth century and afterwards, so that we can appreciate (in the next chapter) the depth and quality of the orthodox Christology of the Ecumenical Councils of Ephesus, Chalcedon and Constantinople II and III.

APOLLINARIANISM

At the Council of Constantinople (381), Apollinarianism was declared to be a heresy and anathematized (Canon 1). A year later the local synod of Constantinople, recalling the earlier Ecumenical Council, declared: "We preserve undistorted the doctrine of the Incarnation of the Lord, holding the tradition that the dispensation (economy) of the flesh is neither without soul nor without mind nor imperfect; and knowing full well that the Word of God was perfect before the ages and became perfect man in the last days for our salvation."

Apollinarianism takes its name from Apollinarius, Bishop of Laodicea (c. 310-390), who was a friend of Athanasius and a strong supporter of the Nicene *homoousios*. At the same time, he was vehemently opposed to any presentation of the Incarnate Son which gave the impression that Jesus Christ was really not one Person but a union of two—the Son of God joined to the son of Mary. He emphasized that Jesus Christ is a unity not a binity or duality. He is One Person not two! Unless he is truly One Person, the Incarnate Son of God, how can he be the Savior of the world?

There is always the danger that in opposing one error the enthusiast will espouse another error simply by over-emphasizing an important truth. In his opposition to what we may call a dualist or Word-Man Christology, Apollinarius spoke of the "flesh-bearing God." His Christology belongs to the Word-flesh type, for he believed that the eternal Word took to himself a human body, that is human flesh and blood. Significantly, he did not believe that the Incarnation included the taking of a human, rational soul, since he judged that the Word supplied all that which (in a normal man) is regarded as human psychology—the existence and activity of the mind, emotions and will. The energy of the Word fulfills in Jesus Christ, said Apollinarius, both the role of life-giver to the flesh and of the activating of the human mind and will. Thus, Jesus Christ does not have a rational soul and in this he is not truly a man—not even like Adam before the fall into sin.

So there is a unity of nature between the Word and his fleshly body, said the Bishop of Laodicea. Further, since the Word supplies the vital force and energy within the one Lord Jesus Christ, he was able to raise the dead and heal the sick. In no way, said Apollinarius, can the incarnate Lord be one Person with two natures: he is one Person with one nature because the flesh has no independence whatsoever—it is wholly energized and moved by the Word himself. The flesh is truly the flesh of the Word and has no life apart from him. As it was assumed and taken by the Word in the womb of the Virgin Mary, the flesh was deified and divinized, but it remained human flesh.

What Apollinarius refused to say was that in Jesus Christ there was not only a human body, flesh and blood, but also a human soul (mind, emotions and will). To have said that the Incarnation involved the taking of a total human nature and body would have been for him to say that the eternal Son joined to himself a man—and such teaching was a horror to him. Apollinarius solemnly believed that he was preserving the teaching of the Creed of Nicea, and that the Christ he proclaimed alone could be truly the Savior of the world and the true life-giver through his sacramental body and blood in the Eucharist.

The heresy of Apollinarius consisted in the single affirmation that the divine spirit of the Word was substituted in the Lord Jesus Christ for a human mind. When he said that God took flesh or God took a body, he meant exactly that and no more! Apollinarius could not see how two minds and two principles of action could co-exist in an individual, living being. If the Son of God did not supply the immaterial, spiritual and rational consciousness of the body/flesh, then, he concluded, Jesus Christ was two Sons.

Further, Apollinarius held that the spiritual, rational consciousness of mankind had been fatally diseased and corrupted through its association with, and subservience to, the sinful flesh.

In short, a human mind is subject to change and is the captive of filthy imaginations. Therefore, if there is to be redemption, a new type of mind had to become available within man, and it was this mind that came into the world in the Son of God. Apollinarianism—the teaching of both Apollinarius and his varied disciples—was condemned by the orthodox Fathers and by the Council of Constantinople for several reasons. First and foremost, the picture it presented of Jesus did not match what was being read in the churches from the Gospels each week. As presented by the four evangelists, Jesus had real human nature and manhood. He did not merely *seem* to be a man, he *was* a real man, who acted and talked as men do—even though he was without sin. In the second place, the salvation this system offered was not a full and complete salvation because the Savior was not a full and complete man. In the oft-quoted words of Gregory of Nazianzus: "What has not been assumed cannot be restored" (*Epistle,* 101, 7.). A half-human Savior is only useful for a half-fallen Adam. The mind of man needed redemption more than his body. When Adam disobeyed God and thereby introduced sin into the human race, Adam sinned in his soul (mind and will) and then in his flesh. Thus, the Incarnate Word as the New and Second Adam had to assume, and make his very own, a human soul if he were truly to be the Savior of sinful men.

NESTORIANISM

At the Ecumenical Council of Ephesus (431), Nestorius and his teaching were condemned. Nestorius, Bishop of Constantinople from 428, was an eloquent preacher, who spoke against the title, *Theotokos*, being given to the Virgin Mary because he believed that it led inexorably towards the heresy of Apollinarianism. Though summoned to attend the Council in Ephesus he refused, and in his absence he was condemned. Later, the Emperor Theodosius agreed to his removal from Constantinople and for his writings to be burned.

The condemnation of Nestorius by the Council was made in the following words:

> **As, in addition to other things, the most honorable Nestorius has not obeyed our citation and did not receive the holy Bishops who were sent by us to him, we were compelled to examine his ungodly doctrines. We discovered that he had held and published impious doctrines in his letters and treatises, as well as in discourses which he delivered in this city, and which have been testified to. Compelled of necessity by the canons and by the letter of our most holy Father and fellow servant Celestine, Bishop of the church of the Romans, we have come, with many tears, to this sorrowful sentence against him—namely that our Lord Jesus Christ, whom he has blasphemed, decrees by this holy Synod that Nestorius be excluded from the episcopal dignity, and from all priestly communion.**

Further, included in the decrees of this Council are a Letter of Cyril to Nestorius, which was approved; a Letter of Nestorius to Cyril, which was condemned; Twelve Anathemas against Nestorianism; and several paragraphs concerning Nestorianism in a Letter of the Council to all Bishops informing them of the condemnation of John of Antioch.

Whether Nestorius was actually a Nestorian has been often discussed by scholars this century—in much the same way as the discussion as to whether Calvin was a Calvinist and Luther a Lutheran! What is clear is that Nestorius used much intemperate and ill-considered language in his preaching and writing against the use of *Theotokos*, giving the impression that Mary bore a mere man, not the Son of God incarnate. As he was heard and read by those for whom the title, *Theotokos*, was precious and necessary, Nestorius appeared to be teaching that there were in fact Two distinct Persons and Sons in Jesus Christ—the Person of the eternal Son and the person of the son of Mary. Thus, Nestorianism has been regarded as the heresy which split the God-Man into Two distinct Persons.

Nestorius insisted that in Jesus Christ were two complete and full natures, the divine and the human. Further, each nature was objectively real and thus, had its own external aspect or form as well as its own subsistence. Thus, the Godhead existed in the man, and the man existed in the Godhead, and in this union there was no confusion or mixing of the two natures. Jesus as the man actually lived a genuine human life, and the eternal Son also had his own genuine, divine and eternal life. However, there was a perfect, exact, voluntary and continuous conjunction of the two natures. That is, the eternal Son in gracious condescension, and the human nature in loving obedience, were drawn together and stayed together, according to the will and purpose of the Father and through the presence and activity of the Holy Spirit. And as a result of this holy union, Jesus Christ was truly a single being with a single will and intelligence, indivisible and inseparable into two beings.

In terms of his outward appearance and form, Jesus Christ was and is one individual person (*prosopon*). Though each nature has its own *prosopon* there is a common *prosopon,* existing because of the union of the divinity and humanity. This common *prosopon* is neither the *prosopon* of the eternal Son, nor the *prosopon* of the manhood, but is a new *prosopon* existing because of the coalescence of the two natures. Even as the eternal Word took upon himself the form of a servant and even as the humanity had the form of Godhead bestowed upon it, so as a result of this holy exchange there emerged the unique *prosopon* of Jesus Christ, the God-Man.

Nestorius' teaching was received by his opponents and interpreted as a doctrine which assumed that Jesus Christ is the union of two Sons and is not therefore a genuine Person. This rather simplified and mistaken account of Nestorius' position was what was known as Nestorianism and condemned by the Council of Ephesus. Between Nestorius and his opponents (militantly led by Cyril of Alexandria), there was a gulf of misunderstanding which included the continual use of the same key words, but with differing meanings (e.g., *hypostasis, prosopon* and *theotokos*), as well as, a different approach to the problems of Christology. This said, the Ecumenical Council of Ephesus has been judged right, both to condemn what it defined as Nestorianism and to uphold the proper use of the title, *Theotokos*, of the Blessed Virgin Mary.

In his excellent account of Nestorius and Nestorianism, G. L. Prestige wrote:

> In principle, Nestorius taught nothing new. His views on the Person of Christ were, as his critics rightly judged, taken in substance from Theodore of Mopsuestia, who died in 428, when he was just embarking on his controversial episcopate [in Constantinople]; and Theodore had only developed the thoughts of Diodore of Tarsus, the enemy of Apollinarius; and Diodore himself had built upon a foundation laid by Eustace of Antioch, who was deprived in the early days of Arianism because he supported Athanasius and the Nicene Creed too vigorously...The characteristic tendency of the whole school was to lay stress on the entire reality and completeness of Christ's human nature...Their recurrent difficulty, which came to a head in the course of the Nestorian controversy, was to reconcile their habitual manner of talking about the God and the man in Jesus Christ with a convincing statement of the union of both in a single person. (*Fathers and Heretics*, p. 131.)

In other words, Nestorius belonged to what has been called the Antiochene Word-Man Christology and gave the impression to his critics that he approached the definition of Jesus Christ only from the duality and never from the unity of his being. In fact, all that Nestorius did was,

> to put a razor-like dialectical edge on Theodore's tools and apply them to the cutting-up of Apollinarianism or anything else that he considered to betray an Apollinarian character (*Ibid.*, p. 141).

Further,

> the real theological bond between all the Antiochenes was their clear perception of the full and genuine human experience which the incarnate Son historically underwent; they shrank in horror from the idea that he was not in all respects as truly kin to us as he was kin to God; they emphasized the Gospel evidence of his human consciousness and moral growth, and would not have it thought that his human life was merely the illusory exhibition on earth of an action which in sphere and method was exclusively celestial (*Ibid.*, p. 133).

So it was that the Antioch school of theology emphasized that there is a single Redeemer, but they were unable to give a satisfactory account of him as a whole. They were heard by others, especially the Alexandrines, as saying that the sum of God and of man is a partnership rather than a single personality (and, in layman's terms, this was the heresy of Nestorianism condemned by the Ecumenical Councils).

Nestorianism was condemned as heresy when Nestorius was alive and well (at Ephesus in 431), but Theodore of Mopsuestia (c.350-428) was condemned by an Ecumenical Council (Constantinople II in 553) as a heretic when he was dead and long buried as a Bishop of the Catholic Church. The fourteen anathemas of the Second Ecumenical Council of Constantinople were directed in general against Nestorianism and specifically against "The Three Chapters" (or "the three headings" or "topics"), the first of which was the person and the writings of Theodore. Politically, the condemnation of "The Three Chapters" was intended by the Emperor Justinian to appease those churchmen who clung tenaciously to the "one incarnate nature" doctrine of Cyril (for which see below) and who are called Monophysites. This, however, did not stop the Nestorians who were now found primarily in Persia looking upon Justinian as "the tyrannical emperor."

A leading theologian of the Nestorians was Babai the Great, who was known as the creator of Nestorian dogmatics. The formula he developed to speak of the Unity and Duality of Jesus Christ, the God-Man, was "two natures, two hypostases, one person of the sonship." Babai was seeking to preserve the dogmatic language of the Holy Trinity where there are three *hypostases* and one of them is the *hypostasis* of the Son. The union of the *hypostasis* of the Son with his divine nature to the manhood (a human hypostasis with a human nature) brings into being the one, and only one, Person of the incarnate Son. Obviously, in using such language the Nestorians were going to find it impossible to agree with either the Chalcedonians or the Monphysites.

EUTYCHIANISM AND MONOPHYSITISM

Eutyches was Archimandrite (monastic superior) of a large monastery in Constantinople and he had influence at the court of the Emperor through the eunuch, Chrysapius. Around 448, he became the focal point of opposition to what was seen as the continuation of Nestorian teaching—that is, Jesus Christ was not only "out of two natures" but also, as the Incarnate Word, he is "of two natures."

Eutyches claimed to hold to the position which Cyril of Alexandria had espoused at the Ecumenical Council of Ephesus (before he accepted from John of Antioch the Formula of Union which stated that Jesus Christ as One Person had two natures); and he knew that his views were shared, and militantly set forth, by the Patriarch of Alexandria, Dioscorus. In a sentence, Eutyches held that "after the birth of our Lord Jesus Christ I worship one nature—that of God made flesh and become man." Thus he had great difficulty in conceding that, as Man, Jesus Christ is "consubstantial with us." In truth, he did not teach Docetism (that Jesus only seemed to be a man) or Apollinarianism, but he did militantly insist that there was only one nature in the one Person, Jesus Christ, after his conception by the Virgin Mary. His unbalanced and erroneous statements came about because he was too zealous in his desire to avoid all stain of Nestorianism, and because he wanted to be faithful to what he believed were the right concepts and vocabulary of the orthodox Cyril.

After examination of his views, Eutyches was condemned and deposed by the Patriarch Flavian and the Synod of Constantinople in November 448. Not unexpectedly, the Archimandrite immediately used his good connections at court to defend himself. He received support from Dioscorus and with his cooperation persuaded the Emperor Theodosius II to summon a Council to examine his condemnation by Flavian. This met at Ephesus in August 449 and was dominated by Dioscorus. Eutyches was acquitted of heresy and reinstated as Archimandrite; the Formula of Union from John and Cyril of 433 was set aside; and the doctrine that the Incarnate Son was of two natures was anathematized. At best, the Church had by official action in a Council gone back to the position held by Cyril before his dialogue with John of Antioch in 431-433; at worst, the Church had by official action in a Council formally rejected an important development of doctrine concerning the Person of Jesus Christ.

It is not surprising that at a Council at Chalcedon two years later, known as the Fourth Ecumenical Council, the decisions of the "Robber Council" of 449 were annulled, and Eutyches was formally condemned. Further, the teaching of the Church that Jesus Christ is "One Person in Two Natures" was clearly set forth (for which see the next chapter). The Bishops clearly rejected both Nestorianism and Eutychianism when, concerning the mystery of the Incarnation, they declared:

For [the Synod] opposes those who would rend the mystery of the dispensation into a duad of Sons; and it banishes from the assembly of priests those who dare to say that the Godhead of the Only-begotten is passible; and it

124

> **resists those who imagine a mixture or confusion of the two natures of Christ; and it drives away those who fancy that the form of a servant taken by him of us is of a heavenly or any other substance (ousia); and it anathematizes those who, first idly talk of the natures of the Lord as "two before the union" and then conceive but one "after the union."**

The last part is, of course, directly aimed at Eutychianism, which was seen by the Council as a false interpretation of the teaching of Cyril of Alexandria of blessed memory. The latter's position was that "after the union" there is "one *incarnate* nature of the divine Word." Eutychianism as such did not include the *incarnate* before the word "nature," or if it did, it failed to see that this expression was only valuable (strictly speaking only true) when used against Nestorianism; further, Eutychianism rejected the clarification of terms and development of doctrine accepted by Cyril and set forth in his agreement with John of Antioch (see chapters two and nine for the text of the Formula of Union).

The decrees of the Council of Chalcedon certainly did not cause those who, since that time, have been called Monophysites (from *monos*, one, and *physis*, nature) to cease to teach Monophysitism. The latter term covers both a moderate and an extreme form of the teaching (and all points in between) that the Incarnate Son, Jesus Christ, is "one incarnate nature."

Apart from Eutychianism in the fifth century, the most extreme form of Monophysitism was that taught by Julian, Bishop of Halicarnassus in Caria, and his supporters, the "Julianists," in the first part of the sixth century. These held that from the moment of conception the body of the Incarnate Word was both incorruptible and immortal and so they were also called "Aphthartodocetae" ("teachers of the incorruptibility of the Body of Christ") and "Phantasiastae" ("teachers of a merely phenomenal Body of Christ").

A more moderate form of Monophysitism was taught by Severus, Patriarch of Antioch, in the early sixth century. He appears to have been opposed primarily to the language of the Council of Chalcedon and desired to do justice to the humanity of Christ without speaking of it as a distinct and separate "nature."

What most of those who rallied to the monophysite cause after the Council of Chalcedon held in common was a criticism of the Definition of Faith from that Council under three headings. They believed that the Definition should have included the formula of Cyril, "one incarnate nature of the divine Logos." They also held that the Definition should have spoken clearly of "the hypostatic union" in the One Christ; and, finally, they held that the Definition should have declared that the Incarnate Son is "out of two natures" but not of, or in, two natures. The fact that it did not state these "received truths," they further held, showed that it was both Nestorian and out of line with holy Tradition from Athanasius and Cyril. In short, it was in error!

We must realize that there was a real problem with terminology which exacerbated the differences in understanding. "Two natures" was an impossible phrase for the Monophysites. Timothy, the Patriarch of Constantinople (511-517), and a moderate Monophysite, wrote *A Refutation of the Synod of Chalcedon*, in which he asserted:

> There is no nature (=*substantia*) which has not its *hypostasis*, and there is no *hypostasis* which exists without its *prosopon*; if then there are two natures, there are of necessity two *prosopa*; but if there are two *prosopa*, there are also two Christs, as these new teachers [the Chalcedonians] teach. (Cited by R. V. Sellers, *The Council of Chalcedon*, p. 260.)

In other words, for Monophysitism there is no nature without a distinct person and neither is there a distinct person without a nature. Thus, if there are two real natures there must be two distinct Persons and thus Two Sons, the Son of God and the son of Mary. Timothy also wrote:

> No one, whose heart is sound in the Faith has ever taught or upheld two natures before or after the union. For the divine Logos, not yet incarnate, was conceived in the womb of the holy Virgin, and was then incarnate of the flesh of the holy Virgin, in a manner which he alone knew, while remaining without change and without conversion as God; and he is one with the flesh. In fact the flesh had neither *hypostasis* nor *ousia* before the conception of God the Logos, that it equally could be called a nature, separate and existing by itself. (*Ibid.*, p. 262.)

Before the union there was one *hypostasis* of the Logos and after the union there was one *hypostasis*, though now it is the incarnate *hypostasis* of the Logos.

At the Fifth Ecumenical Council of Constantinople in 553, certain Monophysite ideas and phrases were given a place in the Orthodox tradition, but only within the preservation of the teaching of Chalcedon. Here is the eighth anathema where "out of two natures" and "one incarnate nature of God the Word" occur in a positive sense:

> **If anyone who confesses that the union was effected out of two natures, deity and humanity, or speaks of one incarnate nature of God the Word, does not so take these terms, as the holy Fathers taught, that out of the divine nature and the human, when the union by *hypostasis* took place, one Christ was formed, but out of these phrases tries to introduce one nature or substance of the Godhead and flesh of Christ, let him be anathema. For when saying that the Only-begotten Word was united by *hypostasis*, we do not mean that there was any mixture of the natures with each other, but rather we think of the Word**

**as united with flesh, each remaining what it is. Therefore
Christ is one, God and man, the same consubstantial with
the Father in Godhead, and the same consubstantial with
us in manhood. Equally, therefore, does the Church of
God reject and anathematize those who divide into parts
or cut up, and those who confuse, the mystery of the divine dispensation of Christ.**

The anathema closes by condemning not only extreme
Monophysitism, but also Nestorianism.

MONOTHELITISM

In the seventh century, there arose a new form of
Monophysitism, produced with the intention of allowing the
moderate Monophysites to unite with the Chalcedonians when
the Empire was under threat from invasion by Persians and
Muslims. In 624 in the reign of the Emperor Heraclius, theologians came up with what seemed a compromise acceptable to
both sides—that the Incarnate Son had two natures but only
one mode of activity (Greek *mia energeia*). This new approach
seemed to be very successful, being approved by Sergius, Patriarch of Constantinople, and the Bishop of Rome, Pope
Honorius, who actually wrote that in Jesus Christ there is "one
will." So Sergius went ahead and composed a document known
as the *Ekthesis* ("Statement of Faith") in which it was asserted
that the two natures were united in a single Will in the One
Christ.

Thus Monothelitism (from *monos*, one, and *thelein*, to will)
was born and the *Ekthesis* was its Charter! It was approved by
two Councils held in Constantinople in 638 and 639. Later,
however, the *Ekthesis* was disowned by leading bishops and so
in 648 the Emperor Constans II withdrew it and replaced it
with another document, an imperial edict known as the *Typos*
("Example" or "Figure"), in which he forbad anyone to speak

either of "One Will" or "Two Wills" (Dyothelitism) in the Incarnate Son, and to keep to the terminology of the five Ecumenical Councils.

The controversy, however, proceeded for another thirty or so years until the Sixth Ecumenical Council, held in Constantinople in 680-681. This Synod clearly stated that the orthodox faith is that there are not only two natures but also two wills in the one Lord Jesus Christ. Honorarius, the Pope who had first used the expression "one will," Sergius, the Patriarch of Constantinople, and others who had taught that there is only one operation (energy) and only one will in Jesus Christ, were anathematized by this Council. They had attempted, said the Bishops in Council, to **"destroy the perfection of the Incarnation of the Lord Jesus Christ, our God, by blasphemously representing his flesh endowed with a rational soul as devoid of all will or operation."** Thus, they had effectively made his manhood into an imperfect manhood.

FOR FURTHER READING

J. N. D. Kelly, *Early Christian Doctrines,* rev. ed. (San Francisco: Harper, 1981) is always valuable for teaching of the first five centuries. G. L. Prestige, *Fathers and Heretics* (London: SPCK, 1948) provides excellent expositions of Apollinarianism and Nestorianism. John Meyendorff, *Christ in Eastern Christian Thought* (Crestwood, NY: St. Vladimir's Seminary Press, 1975) provides important insights into Christology in the East after the Council of Chalcedon (451). Also Jaroslav Pelikan, *The Spirit of Eastern Christendom (600-1700)* (Chicago: University of Chicago Press, 1974) has a long and valuable chapter on Christology (Chalcedonian, Nestorian and Monophysite) from the fifth to the seventh century (pp. 37-90). For the story up to the fifth century there is the splendid work of Aloys Grillmeier, *Christ in Christian Tradition: From the Apostolic Age to Chalcedon (451)* (Atlanta: John Knox Press, 1975). Then there is W. H. C. Frend, *The Rise of the Monophysite Movement* (Cambridge: Cambridge University Press, 1972) whose history of the early Church, *The Rise of Christianity*, we have already commended for general introductory reading. For more detail on the Christology of Monophysitism see Robert C. Chesnut, *Three Monophysite Christologies: Severus of Antioch, Philoxenus of Mabbug and Jacob of Sarug* (Oxford: Oxford University Press, 1976).

CHAPTER NINE

Orthodoxy Affirmed—
One Person in Two Natures

S t. Paul declared that "God was in Christ, reconciling the world to himself," (II Cor. 5:19). The central problem of Christology in the early Church was to maintain the true humanity and manhood of the Savior, without in any way obscuring the fact that the Second Person of the Trinity, the eternal Son, *homoousios* with the Father, was truly present and active on earth as Jesus Christ.

THE CHRISTOLOGY OF ATHANASIUS AND CYRIL

Athanasius, whose crucial contribution to the development of the dogma of the Holy Trinity we have noted, interpreted John 1:14 ("the Word became flesh") to mean that the Logos actually became man, not that the Logos entered into a man. His exposition of the identity of Jesus Christ is wholly of the Word-flesh rather than Word-Man type. Thus it has sometimes been supposed that, like Apollinarius, he did not recognize in the "flesh" of Jesus Christ a human soul. However, as the chairman of the important Synod of Alexandria in 362, which provided clarity of terminology for the doctrine of the Trinity, he did agree to this formula:

> The Savior did not have a body lacking a soul, sensibility or intelligence. For it was impossible that, the Lord having become man on our behalf, his body should have been without intelligence, and the salvation not only of the body but of the soul as well was accomplished through the Word himself. (Cited by Kelly, *Early Christian Doctrines*, p. 288, from the *Tome to Antioch*, 7.)

It is possible that, towards the end of his life, as his mind turned from the exposition of the doctrine of the Trinity to the consideration of the truth concerning the actual Incarnate Son, that Athanasius began to take more seriously the need to do full justice to the actual and real manhood of the Savior.

Dr. Prestige has remarked that Athanasius "was so thoroughly preoccupied with the thought of God in Christ reconciling the world to himself that he retained little interest in Christ as a distinctive human being, and disregarded the importance of his human consciousness" (*Fathers and Heretics*, p. 115). Of course, this is not to say that Athanasius was an Apollinarian! The general flavor of the Christology of Athanasius may be seen in this extract from his fourth Letter to Serapion (chapter 14), where after citing two oft-quoted texts (John 1:14 and Phil. 2:6-7), the great stalwart of Trinitarian Orthodoxy wrote:

> Therefore, since God he is and man he became, as God he raised the dead and, healing all by a word, also changed the water into wine. Such deeds were not those of a man. But as wearing a body he thirsted and was wearied and suffered; these experiences are not characteristic of the deity. And as God he said, "I am in the Father and the Father in me;" but as wearing a body he rebuked the Jews, "Why do you seek to kill me, a man that told you the truth which I heard from

the Father?" But these facts did not occur in dissociation, on lines governed by the particular quality of the several acts, so as to ascribe one set of experiences to the body apart from the deity and the other to the deity apart from the body. They all occurred interconnectedly, and it was the one Lord who did them all wondrously by his own grace. For he spat in a human fashion, yet his spittle was charged with deity, for therewith he caused the eyes of the man born blind to recover their sight; and when he willed to declare himself God it was with a human tongue that he signified this saying, "I and the Father are one." And he used to perform cures by a mere act of will. But he stretched forth a human hand to raise Peter's wife's mother when she was sick of a fever, and to raise up from the dead the daughter of the ruler of the synagogue when she had already expired. (translated by G. L. Prestige, *Ibid.*, p. 179.)

It was for Cyril, a later Patriarch of Alexandria, to refine this Word-flesh Christology so that it could become Church dogma at the Council of Ephesus (431).

Those who taught the Word-flesh Christology did not approach the identity of Jesus Christ by beginning from the union in him of two different natures, human and divine—as the Antiochene school tended to do. They thought of two phases within the existence of God the Word—one before and one after the Incarnation. The Logos who existed outside and apart from flesh became enfleshed and embodied by his Incarnation. Therefore, Cyril and many others after him spoke of "one nature, and that incarnate, of the divine Word." It is important to appreciate that, as used in this statement, "nature" (*physis*) is being used to mean "concrete, individual, independent existent" or, as Dr. Prestige suggests, "a concrete personality."

The basic meaning of *physis* is the way in which a thing grows and functions—hence its nature. Also it can mean, as a development from this, the actual thing that grows and functions. Cyril used *physis* in the latter sense, meaning a concrete personality. The *physis* of God the Word is for Cyril the Word himself, the personal subject of all his actions, words and experiences. [In contrast, as used by the Antiochenes (with whom Cyril did theological battle), *physis* takes as its primary meaning the way in which a thing grows and functions—hence for them *physis* is "a concrete assemblage of characteristics and attributes." So they could happily speak of two natures, one divine and one human, in the One Lord Jesus Christ and in so doing could horrify the Alexandrians. It hardly needs to be added that they also were horrified to hear from Cyril that the Incarnate Son was of only one nature!]

Cyril was careful to avoid falling into the error of Apollinarius and thus he always insisted that "flesh" means "human nature with a soul" and thus, the Logos as enfleshed had a human soul. As he told Nestorius in his Second Letter, which is part of the Decrees of the Council of Ephesus (431):

We do not say that the nature of the Word was changed and became flesh, or that it converted into a whole man consisting of soul and body; but rather that the Word having personally united to himself flesh animated by a rational soul, did in an ineffable and inconceivable manner become man, and was called the Son of Man...He who had an existence before all ages and was born of the Father, is said to have been born according to the flesh of a woman, not as though his divine nature received its beginning of existence in the holy Virgin, for it needed not any second generation after that of the Father...but since, for us and for our salvation, he personally united to himself an human body, and came forth of a woman, he is in this way said to be born after the flesh; for he was not first born a common man of the holy Virgin, and then the Word came down and entered into him, but the union being made in the womb itself, he [the Word] is said to endure a birth after the flesh, ascribing to himself the birth of his own flesh.

For Cyril, as he emphasized later in this Letter, it was the Logos who took and was made flesh. Therefore, Christians must not divide the One Lord Jesus Christ into Two Sons!

This expression, "The Word was made flesh," can mean nothing else, said Cyril, but that he partook of flesh and blood like to us; he made our body his own, and came forth man from a woman, not casting off his existence as God, or his generation of God the Father, but even in taking to himself flesh remaining what he was.

In this light, he insisted that the Blessed Virgin is truly *Theotokos*, the "God-bearer," since her Son is none other than God the Word. In fact, the first anathema of the twelve contained in his Third Letter to Nestorius states:

> **If anyone does not confess that Emmanuel is God in truth, and therefore the holy Virgin is Theotokos—for she bore in the flesh the Word of God become flesh—let him be anathema.**

From this perspective of the Logos-flesh Christology, wherein there is one incarnate nature of the God the Word, Cyril could neither appreciate nor tolerate what is known as Nestorianism. He used the same fervor to attack it as his predecessors had employed to attack the essentially paganized doctrine of Arius. Thus, he was primarily responsible for the anathematizing of Nestorianism at the Council of Ephesus (431). The fourth anathema goes to the heart of what was deemed to be the error of Nestorianism:

> **If anyone distributes between two persons or hypostases the terms used in the Gospels or in the apostolic writings, whether spoken of Christ by the holy writers or by him about himself, and attaches some to a man thought of separately from the Word of God, and others, as befitting God, to him as to the Word from God the Father, let him be anathema.**

The final anathema shows both how Cyril understood the sufferings and death of Christ and how, by implication, he understood Nestorius and what some Antiochenes were teaching:

> **If anyone does not confess that the Word of God suffered in the flesh and was crucified in the flesh and tasted death in the flesh, and became [by Resurrection] the first-born from the dead—although he is as God Life and Life-giving—let him be anathema. He who was crucified was not a Man conjoined to the Word but the very Word himself in his human nature and body.**

At first John, Patriarch of Antioch, supported Nestorius but later, when he realized that the Emperor as well as the Bishop of Rome accepted the Word-flesh Christology of Cyril approved by the Council of Ephesus (431), he changed his approach. He wrote a doctrinal statement, which has been called "The Formula of Union," which was taken from Antioch to Alexandria by Bishop Paul of Emesa. Here it was accepted by Cyril and copied into a Letter which Cyril then wrote to John. Here is the substance of it:

> **We confess, therefore, our Lord Jesus Christ, the only begotten Son of God, perfect God and perfect man composed of a rational soul and a body, begotten before the ages from his Father in respect of his divinity, but likewise in these last days for us and for our salvation from Mary the Virgin in respect of his manhood; consubstantial with the Father in respect of his divinity and at the same time consubstantial with us in respect of his manhood. For a union of two natures has been accomplished. Hence we confess one Christ, one Son, one Lord. According to this understanding of the union without confusion, we confess the holy Virgin to be the Mother of God [*Theotokos*] because the divine Word became flesh and was made man and from the very conception united to himself the temple taken from her. As for the evangelical**

and apostolic statements about the Lord, we recognize that theologians employ some indifferently in view of the unity of person, but distinguish others in view of the duality of natures, applying the God-befitting ones to Christ's divinity and the lowly ones to his humanity.

Obviously, this Formula seeks to preserve certain Antiochene insights (e.g., the calling of the human nature "the temple taken from her" and the acceptance of "a duality of natures") within a general Alexandrine theology (e.g. the Virgin is *Theotokos*). As a theological Statement it certainly paved the way for the Definition on the Person of Christ from the Council of Chalcedon (451), but it also angered those of the Word-flesh school for whom there was no negotiation over their fixed belief in "the one incarnate nature of God the Word."

THE CHRISTOLOGY OF LEO

What Pope Leo I saw as the exaggerated Monophysitism of Eutyches, led to his writing what is called *The Tome of Leo* (= his twenty-eighth Letter) addressed to Flavian, Patriarch of Constantinople. Though this masterful Letter was rejected by the "Robber Council" of Ephesus in 449, it did become part of the decrees of the Ecumenical Council of Chalcedon in 451. We must note its theological content, using the translation of William Bright in *Select Sermons of St. Leo . . . with his Twenty-Eighth Epistle, called the Tome* (1886).

Leo began by pointing out that if Eutyches had truly understood the meaning of the baptismal Creed, he would not have espoused and taught the grievous error that the body of the Savior was not derived from his mother's body. Then he continued:

For it was the Holy Ghost who gave fecundity to the Virgin, but it was from a body that a real body was derived;

and when "Wisdom was building herself a house" (Prov. 9:1), "the Word was made flesh and dwelt among us" (John 1:14), that is, in that flesh which he assumed from a human being, and which he animated with the spirit of rational life.

Leo is clear that the flesh of the Savior is full human nature. It was not a nature brought down from heaven or a diluted or depleted form of human nature taken from the Virgin Mary.

In chapter 3, Leo explained how Jesus Christ is One Person with Two Natures:

Accordingly, while the distinctness of both natures and substances is preserved, and both meet in one Person, lowliness is assumed by majesty, weakness by power, mortality by eternity; and in order to pay the debt of our condition, the inviolable nature has been united to the passible, so that, as the appropriate remedy for our ills, one and the same "Mediator between God and men, the man Christ Jesus" (I Tim. 2:5) might from one element be capable of dying, and from another be incapable. Therefore, in the entire and perfect nature of very Man was born very God, whole in what was his, whole in what was ours.

In taking what was ours he did not take our sin, but human nature as it existed in Adam before his disobedience and sin. That is, he took on him "the form of a servant" without the defilement of sins. As the Invisible he made himself visible, and as the Lord of all, he willed to be one among mortal men.

In chapter 4, the meaning of the Incarnation is further developed in this manner:

Accordingly, the Son of God, descending from his seat in heaven, yet not departing from the glory of the Father, enters this lower world, born after a new order, by a new mode of birth. After a new order, because he who in his

own sphere is invisible became visible in ours; he who could not be enclosed in space willed to be enclosed; continuing to be before times, he began to exist in time; the Lord of the universe allowed his infinite Majesty to be overshadowed, and took upon him the form of a servant; the impassible God did not disdain to become passible, and the immortal One to be subject to the laws of death. And born by a new mode of birth, because inviolate virginity, while ignorant of concupiscence, supplied the matter of his flesh.

What was assumed from the Lord's mother was nature, not fault; and the fact that the nativity of our Lord Jesus Christ is wonderful, in that he was born of a Virgin's womb, does not imply that his nature is unlike ours. For the selfsame who is very God is also very Man: and there is no illusion in this union, while the lowliness of man and the loftiness of Godhead meet together. For as "God" is not changed by the compassion [exhibited], so "Man" is not consumed by the dignity [bestowed]. For each "form" does the acts which belong to it, in communion with the other; the Word, that is, performing what belongs to the Word, and the flesh carrying out what belongs to the flesh. The one of these shines out in miracles; the other succumbs to injuries.

And as the Word does not withdraw from equality with the Father in glory, so the flesh does not abandon the nature of our kind. For, as we must often be saying, he is one and the same, truly Son of God, and truly Son of Man: God, inasmuch as "in the beginning was the Word and the Word was with God and the Word was God;" Man, inasmuch as "the Word was made flesh and dwelt among us." God, inasmuch as "all things were made by him, and without him nothing was made" (John 1:1, 14, 3,); Man, inasmuch as he was "made of a woman, made under the law" (Gal. 4:4).

Chapter 4 ends with this important sentence concerning the unity of the Person of Jesus Christ, God and Man.

> **For although in the Lord Jesus Christ there is one Person of God and man, yet that whereby contumely attaches to both is one thing, and that whereby glory attaches to both is another: for from what belongs to us he has that manhood which is inferior to the Father; while from the Father he has equal Godhead with the Father.**

And chapter 5 begins with another statement concerning the reality and mystery of Jesus Christ, who is One Person with two natures.

> **Accordingly, on account of the unity which is to be understood as existing in both the natures, we read, on the one hand, that "the Son of Man came down from heaven" (John 3:13), inasmuch as the Son of God took flesh from the Virgin of whom he was born; and, on the other hand, the Son of God is said to have been crucified and buried (I Cor. 2:8), inasmuch as he underwent this, not in his actual Godhead, wherein the Only-begotten is coeternal and consubstantial with the Father, but in the weakness of human nature.**

Here we have Leo's use of what in theology is called the *communicatio idiomatum* ("interchange of the properties"). In this approach, Leo was identifying with Cyril of Alexandria and teaching that while the divinity and humanity of the Lord Jesus are separate, the attributes of one may be predicated of the other in view of their union in the One Person of the Savior.

The Christology of Leo may be summarized in four points. First of all, the Person of the God-Man is identical with the Person of the Word of God. Secondly, in this One Person, the divine and human natures exist without mixture or confusion. In the third place, each nature is a separate sphere of operation although the two natures always act in perfect unity. Finally, the oneness of the Person legitimates and requires the communication of idioms or properties between the two natures.

It may be said that Leo's theology is in agreement with the best intentions of the Antiochene Word-Man theology, but is more exact. Leo used the word "nature" (Latin, *natura*) not in the way used by Cyril and the Alexandrine School as synonymous with *hypostasis*, but with the general meaning of "a concrete assemblage of characteristics or attributes" as used in Antioch. On the other hand, Leo was one with Cyril and Alexandria in insisting on the identity of the Person of the pre-existent, eternal Word and the Word incarnate.

CHALCEDONIAN CHRISTOLOGY

In the Council, the Bishops reaffirmed both the Creed of the 318 Fathers (325) and the Creed of the 150 Fathers (381). They canonized Cyril's Letters to Nestorius and John of Antioch (found in the decrees of Ephesus, 431) as containing orthodox teaching and rejecting Nestorianism. Also, they canonized Leo's *Tome* as overthrowing Eutychianism and confirming the true doctrine of Jesus Christ.

Further, after much debate and research, the Bishops produced their own Definition of the Faith, of which the central portion is itself usually called by the name which belongs to the whole. To understand this central portion we shall divide it into two paragraphs. The first is primarily concerned with the unity of the Person of Christ, while the second sets forth the reality of his two natures.

The literary and doctrinal sources of the first paragraph are the Formula of Union between Cyril and John from 433 and the Archbishop Flavian's confession of faith to the Home Synod in Constantinople in November 448.

Following, then, the holy Fathers, we all with one voice teach that it should be confessed that our Lord Jesus Christ is one and the same Son, the same perfect in

> Godhead, the Same perfect in manhood, truly God and truly man, the Same consisting of a rational soul and body; consubstantial [*homoousios*] with the Father as to his Godhead, and the Same consubstantial [*homoousios*] with us as to his manhood; in all things like unto us, sin only excepted; begotten of the Father before the ages as to his Godhead, and in the last days, the Same, for us and for our salvation, of the Virgin Mary, Mother of God [*Theotokos*], as to his manhood.

What is important to notice here is the repeated occurrence of "the Same," by which the truth that the Son, who was with the Father in all eternity is the one and the same Son who was with us as the Incarnate God, is underlined. In fact, in their differing ways both East and West had emphasized this truth. Further, both East and West had also insisted that the Son of God in his Incarnation really and truly became Man.

It would be wrong, however, to assume that this Statement outlawed and condemned the phrases of the orthodox Alexandrines—that is, "one incarnate nature" and the "hypostatic union." Since these phrases are in the Letters of Cyril canonized by the Council, it is to be assumed that they are legitimate expressions, if interpreted via this Definition of Faith. Certainly, this is the approach taken by the defenders of orthodoxy in later centuries.

We turn now to the second paragraph where the general influence of Cyril's Letters and Leo's Tome are also to be recognized.

> [We confess] One and the same Christ, Son, Lord, Only-begotten, made known in two natures which exist without confusion, without change, without division, without separation; the difference of the natures having been in no wise taken away by reason of the union, but rather the properties of each being preserved, and [both] concurring into one Person [*prosopon*] and one hypostasis—

not parted or divided into two Persons [*prosopa*], but one and the same Son, Only-begotten, the divine Word, the Lord Jesus Christ; even as the prophets from of old have spoken concerning him, and as the Lord Jesus Christ himself has taught us and the Creed of our Fathers has handed down.

He who is "one and the same Son" is "made known in two natures." That is, the One Lord Jesus Christ is shown forth, declared, and presented as well as recognized, understood and acknowledged in the two elements of real Godhead and real manhood. And each of these natures or elements in him has its own properties. Further, each exists in integrity—as the four "withouts" make very clear. The use of the preposition "in" with respect to the two natures reflects the contribution of the West as to the reality of the two natures in the One Christ. However, its use does not automatically or necessarily exclude the Alexandrine emphasis that the incarnate Son is "out of" two natures, when the "out of" is expounded in right relation to the "in."

To express the oneness of the Person of the Lord Jesus Christ the two words, *prosopon* and *hypostasis*, are used. To express the elements or natures of Godhead and manhood, the word *physis* is used. Thus, Christ is One Person in two natures. The Incarnate Son is a single Person and a single subsistent Being; he is not parted or divided into two persons or beings even though he has two natures. Here the terminology is clear, even though it will not be accepted by all in the East in the centuries after this Council. The distinctive theology of this Definition is the equal recognition it gives both to the unity and the duality of the Incarnate Word, the Lord Jesus Christ.

Perhaps a few words of explanation at this point concerning *prosopon* and *hypostasis* will be useful. Originally *prosopon* meant "face" or "countenance" and is used in the Septuagint of the face of Yahweh. Also, it had the meaning of the actor's mask and the role he plays. Obviously, as used in Theology

143

and Christology the word has a developed meaning of a distinct person (Latin *persona*), who has a genuine role and who is in relations with others. Modern notions of personality are, of course, not contained within the word at this stage. They came much later.

Hypostasis, which once approximated to *ousia* in meaning, pointed in later Christian discourse to specific realization or expression as a particular reality. It was a concrete realization of that which is. As used by the Cappadocians in the fourth century, it pointed to concrete, perceptible unity—the unity of the complex of individual and particularizing characteristics. So it closely approached the term *prosopon* in meaning and is used alongside it in statements of faith. Its Latin equivalent was *subsistentia* (subsistence).

In his summary of the achievement of the Council of Chalcedon, J. N. D. Kelly comments on the common charge that the content of the Definition was a triumph of Antiochene and Western teaching:

> Chalcedon is often described as the triumph of the Western, and with it of the Antiochene, Christology. It is true, of course, that the balanced position attained long since in the West and given expression in Leo's Tome, gave the Fathers a model of which they made good use. It is true, also, that without Rome's powerful support the Antiochene formula "two natures" would never have been given such prominence. Further, large sections of the Eastern Church, regarding the Council's endorsement of that formula and of Leo's Tome, as well as its rejection of "hypostatic union," as a betrayal of Cyril and of the Alexandrian tradition generally, were prepared to drift off into schism as Monophysites. These are some of the points that underline the substantial truth of the verdict. It does less than justice, however, to the essential features of Cyril's teaching enshrined, as has been shown, in the Council's confession, especially the recognition, in language of a clarity unheard of in Antiochene circles, of the oneness of Christ and the identity of the Person of the God-

man with that of the Logos. It also overlooks the fact that Cyril's Synodical Letters were given just as honorable a position as the Tome, and greatly exaggerates the theological difference between the two. (*Early Christian Doctrines*, pp. 341-42.)

It can only be claimed that the Antiochene Christology was victorious at Chalcedon if it is understood as an Antiochene Christology which has taken into itself and been modified by the teaching of Cyril.

FROM CHALCEDON TO CONSTANTINOPLE

With Nestorianism pushed beyond the frontiers of the Empire, those who defended the teaching of Chalcedon as the authoritative teaching of the Catholic Church had to do long battle with those who accepted only the first three Councils. Their opponents, the Monophysites, were, of course, fully committed to the orthodox doctrine of the Holy Trinity. However, they could not be persuaded, despite many efforts by emperors and ecclesiastics, that the Definition from Chalcedon was anything but a rejection of the teaching of the authentic Three Councils (Nicea, Constantinople and Ephesus). In their Christology, they clung to the concepts and terminology which they believed were required by the true tradition of the Fathers, and by the need to avoid all taint of Nestorianism with its "Two Sons" theology. Thus, they insisted on using the three expressions—"one incarnate nature of the divine Logos;" "the hypostatic union" and "out of two [natures]"—and seeing in the teaching of Chalcedon the false Antiochene doctrine of the Two Sons.

Chalcedonians attempted to give coherent expositions of the meaning of "One Person in Two Natures." One theologian, whose explanation became part of the tradition of eastern, Orthodox theology, was Leontius of Byzantium (d. 544). His chief work is *Three Books against the Nestorians and Eutychians*. He faced the question of how if there is only one *hypostasis* in

145

Christ there are two natures in him. Monophysites argued that each *hypostasis* has one and one only *physis*. The answer of Leontius was that the manhood or humanity of Christ is neither *anupostatos* (= "uncentered") nor self-centered, but is *enupostatos* (= "encentered") in God. This teaching is called the doctrine of the *enhypostasia*.

The teaching of the Council of Constantinople (553), with its emphatic rejection of Nestorianism and of the Word-Man Christology of Antioch, was in part an attempt to bring on board the ship of Chalcedon the Monophysite leaders. This aim of reconciliation is most obvious in Anathemas 12, 13 and 14 against "the Three Chapters."

Significantly, the first anathema of Constantinople II is against those who deny the received dogma of the Holy Trinity. There is, of course, a clear relation between Theology proper (the doctrine of the Holy Trinity) and Christology (the doctrine of the Person of Christ). As we have observed, the latter was only developed in the Church when the former had been clarified. Further, in the attempt to win over Monophysites, it was good to emphasize first of all what was held in common. Thus the first anathema reads:

> **If anyone does not confess one nature or substance, one power and authority, of the Father, the Son and the Holy Spirit, consubstantial Trinity, one Deity worshipped in three hypostaseis or prosopa, let him be anathema.**

Here we find that the same two words, used of the "one and the same Jesus Christ" at Chalcedon are used of each of the Three of the Holy Trinity. Each is a *hypostasis* and a *prosopon*.

It will be useful to print several of the anathemas (not already printed in chapter eight) to show how the Chalcedonians were accommodating to certain expressions and aspects of the theology of the Monophysites in order both to serve the Truth and to invite reconciliation.

146

Anathema 2

If anyone does not confess that there are two generations of the God the Word, the one before all ages of the Father, without time and without body; the other in these last days when the Word of God came down from heaven and was made flesh of the holy and glorious Mary, Mother of God and ever-virgin, and was born of her: let him be anathema.

Anathema 3

If anyone declares that the Word of God who worked miracles is one Person and the Christ who suffered another, or alleges that God the Word was together with the Christ who was born of woman, or was in him in the way that one might be in another, but that our Lord Jesus Christ was not one and the same, the Word of God incarnate and made man, and that the miracles and the sufferings which he voluntarily endured in the flesh were not of the same Person: let him be anathema.

Anathema 9

If anyone shall take the expression, Christ ought to be worshipped in his two natures, in the sense that he wishes to introduce thus two adorations—the one in special relation to God the Word and the other as pertaining to the man; or if anyone to get rid of the flesh [that is of the humanity of Christ], or to mix together the divinity and the humanity, shall speak monstrously of one only nature or essence of the united (natures), and so worship Christ, and does not venerate by one adoration God the Word made man, together with his own flesh, as the holy Church has taught from the beginning: let him be anathema.

Anathema 10

If anyone does not confess that our Lord Jesus Christ who was crucified in the flesh is true God and the Lord of glory and one of the Holy Trinity: let him be anathema.

Again and again in these anathemas (in 4, 6, 8, 13) it is insisted that the union is truly an "hypostatic union." Further, in this connection, the expression "one incarnate nature of the divine Logos" is allowed.

If there had been any ambiguity in the decrees of Chalcedon (451) about the common *subject* of the two natures and whether this common *subject* is to be described as a *person* before the actual union of the natures had taken place, then that ambiguity was taken away by Constantinople II. The Person, the *prosopon* or *hypostasis* of Christ, is the pre-existent Son and Word of the Father.

If the Second Ecumenical Council to be held in Constantinople (553) had clearly stated the unity of the Person of Christ, then it was the task of the Third Ecumenical Council to be held in Constantinople (680-681) to underline and clarify the duality of natures in the One Person. The theological background to this Council is once again various attempts to reconcile the Monophysites to the Catholic Church. It had been said in these (to which we referred in chapter eight above) that there was in the one Christ only one energy or operation and only one will.

The Bishops in Council stated their commitment to the Creeds of Nicea and Constantinople and to the teaching of all five Ecumenical Councils (Nicea I to Constantinople II), including the Definition of Faith of Chalcedon (451). Then they proceeded by saying:

Following the five holy Ecumenical Councils and the holy and approved fathers, with one voice defining that our

Lord Jesus Christ must be confessed to be very God and very man, one of the holy and consubstantial and life-giving Trinity, perfect in Godhead and perfect in humanity, very God and very man, of a reasonable soul and human body subsisting; consubstantial with the Father as touching his Godhead and consubstantial with us as touching his manhood; in all things like unto us, sin only excepted; begotten of his Father before all ages according to his Godhead, but in these last days for us men and for our salvation made man of the Holy Ghost and of the Virgin Mary, strictly and properly the Mother of God according to the flesh; one and the same Christ our Lord, the only-begotten Son to be acknowledged of two natures which undergo no confusion, no change, no separation, no division, the peculiarities of neither nature being lost by the union, but rather the property of each nature being preserved, concurring in one Person and in one Subsistence, not parted or divided into two persons but one and the same only-begotten Son of God, the Word, our Lord Jesus Christ, according as the prophets of old have taught us and as our Lord Jesus Christ himself hath instructed us, and the Creed of the holy Fathers has delivered to us.

Thus far they repeat the teaching of Chalcedon and of Constantinople II. Then they turn to speak of the concrete, acting personality of the Incarnate Son and state:

We likewise declare that in him are two natural wills and two natural operations which undergo no division, no change, no partition, no confusion, in accordance with the teaching of the holy Fathers. And these two natural wills are not opposed to each other (God forbid!) as the impious heretics assert, but his human will follows and that not as resisting and reluctant, but rather as subject to his divine and omnipotent will. For it was right that the flesh should be naturally moved but subject to the divine will, according to the most wise Athanasius. For

as his flesh is called and is the flesh of God the Word, so also the natural will of his flesh is called and is the proper will of God the Word, as he himself says: "I came down from heaven, not that I might do my own will but the will of the Father which sent me" (John 6:38), where he calls his own will the will of his flesh, inasmuch as his flesh was also his own. For as his most holy and immaculate animated [ensouled] flesh was not destroyed because it was divinized but continued in its own state and nature [literally, "boundary and rule"], so also his human will, although divinized, was not suppressed, but was rather preserved, according to the saying of Gregory the Theologian: "His will, when he is considered in his character as Savior, is not contrary to God but is totally divinized."

We also glorify two natural operations in the same our Lord Jesus Christ, our true God, which undergo no division, no change, no partition, no confusion—that is to say a divine operation and a human operation, according to the divine preacher Leo, who most distinctly asserts: "For each form does in communion with the other what pertains properly to it, the Word, namely, doing that which pertains to the Word, and the flesh that which pertains to the flesh."

For we will not admit the existence of one natural operation of God and the creature, lest we should either take up into the divine nature what is created, or bring down the glory of the divine nature to the place suitable for things that are made.

We recognize the miracles and the sufferings as of one and the same Person, according to the difference of the two natures of which he is, and in which he has his being, as Cyril admirably says.

Preserving, therefore, in every way the "no confusion" and "no division," we set forth the whole confession in

150

> brief: Believing our Lord Jesus Christ, our true God, to be one of the Trinity even after the taking of flesh, we declare that his two natures shine forth in his one *hypostasis* (subsistence), in which he both performed the miracles and endured the sufferings through the whole of his providential dwelling here, and that not in appearance only but in very deed, the difference of nature being recognized in the same one *hypostasis*, by the fact that each nature wills and does the things proper to it, in communion with the other. Wherefore, we glorify two natural wills and two operations, combining with each other in him for the salvation of the human race.

We may note two things in this development of the Chalcedonian doctrine. First, there is the roll-call of the four theologians most obviously associated with the first four Councils—Athanasius, Gregory, Cyril and Leo. Secondly, the union of the two natures and wills in Christ is not presented as a "parallelism" but more of a "synthesis" of the two, which concur in the one *prosopon* of the God-man. As it was later expressed by John of Damascus in his *The Orthodox Faith* (iii. 18), the human will of Christ willed of its own free will those things which the divine will willed it to will.

The Orthodox dogma of the Person of Christ is to be sought in the decrees of the Councils of Ephesus (431), Chalcedon (451) and Constantinople (553 and 680) as these are seen in the context of the dogma of the Holy Trinity set forth at Nicea (325) and Constantinople (381). In today's terms, it is a "Christology from above," for it begins from the assumption that "the Word was made flesh" and "God sent forth his Son, born of a woman."

FOR FURTHER READING

To the books by Meyendorff, Prestige, Kelly, Grillmeier and Pelikan mentioned at the end of chapter eight, one needs to add two books by R. V. Sellers, *The Council of Chalcedon* (London: SPCK, 1953), and *Two Ancient Christologies* (London: SPCK, 1954). The latter compares the Christology of the Schools of Alexandria and Antioch. E. R. Hardy, ed., *Christology of the Later Fathers* (Philadelphia: Westminster Press, 1954), is also very useful for its variety of texts. Leontius and his Chalcedonian doctrine of the *Enhypostasia* is studied in H. M. Relton, *A Study in Christology* (London: 1917). For Eastern Christianity in general, there is A. S. Atiya, *History of Eastern Christianity* (Notre Dame: Notre Dame University Press, 1968) and Donald Attwater, *The Christian Churches of the East,* 2 vols. (Milwaukee: Marquette University Press, 1947-48). Anyone who is particularly interested in the period after the Council of Chalcedon (451) in the East will find fascinating articles on a variety of topics in the journal *The Greek Orthodox Theological Review.*

PART FOUR:

HOLY ICONS

The priest and deacon approach the holy icon of Christ, kiss it, and say,

> "We do homage to thy most pure image, O Good One, entreating forgiveness of our transgressions, O Christ-God; for of thine own good will thou wast graciously pleased to ascend the Cross in the flesh, that thou mightest deliver from bondage to the enemy those whom thou hadst fashioned; With joy hast thou filled all things, O our Savior, in that thou didst come to save the world."

In like manner they also kiss the icon of the Birth-giver of God.

> "O Theotokos, in that thou art a well-spring of loving-kindness, vouchsafe unto us thy compassion. Look upon the people who have sinned. Manifest thy power as ever; for trusting in thee we cry aloud unto thee, Hail! as aforetime did Gabriel, Chief Captain of the heavenly, Bodiless Powers."

[Office of Oblation, Orthodox Liturgy]

CHAPTER TEN

No Graven Images

The earliest Christian art was primarily symbolical. Christ was represented by a fish (Greek *Icthus*) or a young shepherd. The letters of *Icthus* stood for *Iesous Christos, Theou Huios, Soter* (Jesus Christ, Son of God, Savior). The Church was represented as a ship, the hope of salvation by an anchor, and immortality by a peacock. Scenes from Holy Scripture were not merely illustrative but also typical—e.g., Jonah's adventure symbolized death and resurrection.

In the eighth century, both the iconoclasts and iconodules appealed to the sacred text of Holy Scripture (the Septuagint), for both believed it to be the written words of God. They agreed that this Bible uniquely portrays the Word of God incarnate, Jesus Christ, and his Father, who is the invisible, ineffable God of all glory, wisdom and power—the God who is named Yahweh in the Old Testament. Further, they agreed that idolatry, the worship of images, is absolutely condemned in Holy Scripture.

Where they did not see eye to eye was on the distinction between an image (an objectively descriptive word) as an idol (which has a pejorative overtone), and an image as an icon (Greek, *eikon*, an image as representational art). And this disagreement was related to what they took to be the theological implications of the taking of manhood by the Son of God.

Each side agreed that God as Godhead is pure, eternal and ineffable Spirit and cannot under any circumstances be represented in human art. Thus, we shall begin our brief examination of Holy Scripture with the statement of Jesus (often cited by the iconoclasts) that God is Spirit. Then we shall note the condemnation of idolatry and the restricted use of material objects in divine worship in the Old Testament.

GOD IS SPIRIT

In his conversation with the Samaritan woman at the well Jesus said, "God is Spirit" (John 4:24). Some people of a philosophical disposition have supposed that the statement "God is Spirit" is a metaphysical and ontological definition of the eternal nature of the invisible deity. Though God (according to philosophical theism) is eternal, uncreated, pure Spirit, the meaning here has less to do with eternity and more to do with the relation of eternity to space and time. "God is Spirit" is the same general kind of statement as two others found in I John—"God is light" (1:5) and "God is love" (4:8). In all three statements it is God in relation to us, God acting with respect to us, which is being affirmed. John is telling us how the Father really is or truly acts towards us in history on a personal, relational basis.

Jesus is not attempting to speak of God-as-God-is-in-himself (which for Greek Christians is pure theology). His message is of God as God-is-towards-and-for-us (the Trinity in the economy); the Father is the One who gives the Spirit (John 14:16), and it is in and by the Spirit that the Father relates to human beings as his creatures. Therefore, "God [the Father] is Spirit" in the sense that, as the invisible God [who is in himself pure Spirit], he makes himself known through the medium of the Holy Spirit, whom he actually sends into the world.

True worship also is in the sphere of "Spirit." Human beings who worship their Creator and Lord must worship "in spirit [Spirit]," as those who are reborn by water and the Spirit (John

3:5) and who have been baptized with that baptism in the Spirit of which John the Baptist spoke (John 1:33). It is necessary that they worship in this way, for no other approach is acceptable to the Father. Genuine worship must be prompted, energized and brought to fulfillment by the presence and sanctifying power of the Holy Spirit.

And there is a further necessary component! True worship is also "in truth." John's Gospel makes it very clear that the Spirit and the Word (the Son) exist and work in perfect harmony in God's economy of grace. Jesus as the Word (1:1) is also the Truth (14:6), who reveals the very reality of God (8:45; 18:37). In fact, the Spirit is "the Spirit of Truth" (14:17; 15:26; 16:13) in his relation to the Word made flesh. And Jesus is the Truth, who reveals the Father, who does the will of the Father, and who makes access to the Father possible for sinners by his sacrificial death as the Lamb of God. He is the Son of the Father who becomes the man of flesh and blood. Thus true worship must be offered to the Father through (i.e., according to the Truth which is) Jesus and in the Spirit, who is given by the Father and who rests upon and takes from the Son.

It would be false to conclude from John 4:23-24 that worship must only be spiritual, confined to the heart, and without any outward expression of form or ceremony. The apostolic church worshipped through the ministry of Word and Sacrament; and it is highly probable that John 6:53-58 refers to the Eucharist as a primary means of worship. To worship in spirit and in truth is to worship the Trinity by the Trinity. Those who believe on the name of the Son, and who are born from above by the Holy Spirit, worship the Father through the Son and in the Spirit. And they do so because the Father, through the Son and by the Spirit, has not only created them but also revealed himself to them.

God is Spirit and he is also Light. For the apostles, the advent of the Logos, the only Son of the Father, was the coming of light into the world (John 1:4-9; cf. Matt. 4:16; Luke 2:32)—

157

the light shining in darkness. Jesus is *"the* light of the world" while God, the Father, is "light."

> This is the message we have heard from him [Jesus Christ] and proclaim to you, that *God is light and in him is no darkness at all.* If we say we have fellowship with him while we walk in darkness, we lie and do not live according to the truth; but if we walk in the light, as he is in the light, we have fellowship with one another, and the blood of Jesus his Son cleanses us from all sin (I John 1:5-7).

Obviously the Lord our God, as the true and only God, is, of necessity and always, Light both in himself as the transcendent God, and in his relations with the world as its Creator and Redeemer. It is the latter which is in view here. The whole context of I John makes it clear that "God as Light" is not a philosophical, speculative statement about the being and nature of deity, but is a declaration of God's relation to the world as Savior.

In the Old Testament, light is used to symbolize truth in contrast to error, and righteousness in contrast to wickedness (Ps. 36:9; Ps. 119:130; Is. 5:20; Mic. 7:8b). Thus, in Hebrew terms to say that "God is light" is to confess that he is absolute in his glory, in his truth and in his holiness.

The Father is light, the incarnate Son is *the* light, and believers are called to live and walk in the light and have fellowship one with another and with the Father through his only Son. But, we ask, how is this walking and fellowship possible? John answers, "You have been anointed by the Holy One" (I John 2:20; cf. v. 27); that is, you have received the gift of the Holy Spirit. For a man to see the light, to have the light shine in his heart, and to walk in the light, he needs the illumination of the Holy Spirit of light. In other words, Light shines upon and within him from the Father, through the Son and by the Spirit.

God is Spirit, God is Light and God is Love. When we read that "God is love" (I John 4:8) it is the word *agape* which describes God. God is love in that he wills that which is the best for his creatures and he commits himself wholly to achieving this end. Further, it is not only that God is the source of love, but that all of his intentions and activity are loving. We read in I John 4:7-12:

> Beloved, let us love one another; for love is of God, and he who loves is born of God and knows God. He who does not love does not know God; for *God is love*. In this the love of God was made manifest among us, that God sent his only Son into the world so that we might live through him. In this is love, not that we loved God but that he loved us and sent his Son to be the expiation for our sins. Beloved, if God so loved us, we ought also to love one another. No man has ever seen God; if we love one another, God abides in us and his love is perfected in us.

In this paragraph, the verb (*agapeo*) and the noun (*agape*) occur fifteen times. The logic of love is very obvious. God, who is the Father, is love in that he sent his only Son into the world to be the expiation for human sins. "For God so loved the world that he gave his only Son, that whoever believes in him should not perish but have everlasting life" (John 3:16). Yet, God's love is not merely a past determination to do good which was completed by the resurrection of Jesus Christ. God is still love in that his Son, Jesus Christ, was raised from the dead and is alive for evermore, willing the good of all mankind and believers in particular. Further, God is still love in that he abides in those who believe. "By this we know that God abides in us, by the Spirit, which he has given us" (I John 3:24). The Holy Spirit dwells in the souls of the faithful, and it is by his inspiration and power that love is perfected in them and believers are enabled to love one another, thus fulfilling the command of Christ.

The Father loves the Son; the Son loves the Father; and the Holy Spirit is the presence and expression of the love of the Father and the love of the Son. The Father loves the world and sent his only Son into the world; the Son also loves the world and gave himself as a propitiatory and expiatory sacrifice for the sins of the world; the Spirit brings the love of the Father and the Son into the hearts of those who believe, so that they may love God and one another.

In himself as the blessed, holy and undivided Trinity, God is pure Spirit, uncreated Light and holy Love; towards the world and revealed in the incarnate Son, the Trinity is also acting as Spirit, revealing as Light and acting in Love. The Son of the Father become Man is *the Image (eikon)* of God the Father (II Cor. 4:4; Col.1:15). God, who is by nature invisible, comes to visible expression in the incarnate Son. The Son alone is the image of the Father, for as the incarnate Word he is the unique, perfect, material representation of the Father. As the Image of God, Jesus Christ was bodily and physically present with men on earth. As the Image he was seen, heard, touched, and addressed. Therefore, any use by Christians of icons (images) as representational art had to be justified in relation to the Incarnate Son as *the* Image of God.

YAHWEH AND IDOLATRY

Because the Father is ineffable and invisible, and because the incarnate Son is the one and only Image of God, idolatry is wholly forbidden in the New Testament (e.g., I John 5:19-21). This is entirely what we would expect when we recall that in the Old Testament, idolatry is thoroughly condemned by the Law and the Prophets.

"I am the LORD, that is my name; my glory I give to no other, nor my praise to graven images," declared Isaiah (42:8). "I am the LORD your God, who brought you out of the land of Egypt, out of the house of bondage. You shall have no other gods before me. You shall not make yourself a graven image, or any likeness of anything that is in heaven above, or that is in the earth beneath, or that is in the water under the earth; you shall not bow down to them and serve them, for I, the LORD, am a jealous God..." (Ex. 20:2-4).

Three words—LORD, Jehovah and Yahweh—are used in English to render the tetragrammaton, the four Hebrew consonants, YHWH, which is the unique Name of the God of Israel. As this Name was treated with ever more and more reverence, the Jews ceased to pronounce it during the latter part of the Old Testament period. So we are not completely sure today just how it was originally pronounced. "Yahweh" represents the generally accepted modern attempt to recover the original pronunciation of the tetragrammaton.

YHWH is to be taken as a form of the verb *haya*, "to be." In the light of this, it is appropriate to see two meanings arising out of this Name. First of all, from Exodus 3:14-15, YHWH as the Name (revealed to Moses) is a positive assurance of God's acting, aiding and communing presence. The "I AM" will be always with his covenant people. He who is now will be also. In the second place, and based on the declarations of Deuteronomy 4:39, I Kings 8:60 and Isaiah 45:21-22, YHWH is the only God who actually exists and there is no other. YHWH is the one and only Deity, who is both above and within his creation; all other gods are but creatures or the projections of human imagination.

Probably the most well known text in Judaism is the *Shema* of Deuteronomy 6:4-5:

> Hear, O Israel, Yahweh, our Elohim, Yahweh is One, and thou shalt love Yahweh thy Elohim with all thy heart, and with all thy soul and with all thy mind.

Concerning this fundamental confession, Walter Kasper has written:

> The singleness and uniqueness of God is qualitative. God is not only one (*unus*) but also unique (*unicus*); he is as it were

unqualified uniqueness. For by his very nature God is such that there is only one of him. From the nature of God as the reality that determines and includes everything his uniqueness follows with intrinsic necessity. If God is not one, then there is no God. Only one God can be infinite and all inclusive; two Gods would limit one another even if they were somehow interpenetrated. Conversely: as the one God, God is also the only God. The singleness of God is therefore not just one of the attributes of God; rather his singleness is given directly with his very essence. Therefore, too, the oneness and uniqueness of the biblical God is anything but evidence of narrow-mindedness. On the contrary, for precisely as the one and only God, he is the Lord of all peoples and of all history. He is the First and the Last (Is. 41:4; 43:10ff.; 44:6; 48:12; Rev. 1:4, 8, 17). (*The God of Jesus Christ*, pp. 239-40)

Such a living God cannot and must not be presented in images and idols!

Images (normally as idols) were common in Egypt and the ancient near East. They were of two types, either anthropomorphic (in human form) or theriomorphic (in animal form). A molton image was made in a cast from copper, silver or gold. A graven image was carved from stone or wood and wood images could be overlaid with precious metals. Israel was commanded not to worship either an idol of a heathen god(dess) or an image (idol) of Yahweh himself. Thus, alongside the condemnations of idols of heathen gods (Jer. 10:3-5; Hos.11:2) in the Old Testament, there are condemnations of the use of images of Yahweh—the golden calf (Ex. 32:1-8), the image (Ephod) made by Gideon (Judg. 8:26-27), the golden calves of Dan and Bethel (I Kgs. 12:28-30) and the calf of Samaria (Hos. 8:6).

Moses, who personally experienced the glorious and awful presence of Yahweh on the mountain and whose face shone with light as a result of the encounter, recalled the revelation of Yahweh at Mount Sinai when he told the Israelites: "The Lord spoke to you out of the midst of the fire; you heard the sound of words, but saw no form; there was only a voice" (Deut. 4:12). They saw no form and thus they were never to make an image of Yahweh.

The prophets recognized that idols were nothing for they were images of gods who did not exist (Is. 2:8; 40:18-20; 41:6-7; 44:9-20). However, there was more to idolatry than false knowledge. Demonic, evil forces were at work in idolatry and thus the worship of graven and molten images constituted a real spiritual danger (Is. 44:6-20). Thus, an idol is an abomination to Yahweh (Deut. 7:25), and a detested thing (Deut. 29:17; 31:6).

Yet, while the rejection of idolatry is constant and uncompromising in the Law and the Prophets and the Writings (e.g. the Psalter), the religion of Israel was not spiritual in the sense that it was wholly inward, an affair of the human spirit. It was spiritual in that Yahweh was understood to be the transcendent, holy LORD, who was above and beyond the reach of Israel, and who therefore could only be reached when he himself set up the means for communion. This of course he did in what is called the covenant whereby Yahweh was the God of Israel and this people worshipped and served him alone as their God.

Within the means that Yahweh appointed for that spiritual worship and service were physical symbols of his presence and relation to Israel. Here we immediately think of the Tabernacle (Temple) and the Ark of the Covenant (Deut. 10:8), which were constructed through the specific help of the Spirit of Yahweh. The Ark was a rectangular box made of acacia wood, overlaid with gold, whose lid (the "mercy seat") was a gold plate surrounded by two antithetically-placed cherubs with outspread wings. Inside were the two tablets of the Law, a pot of manna and Aaron's rod (Deut. 10:1-5). Yahweh met his people at the Ark. "There I will meet with you, and from above the mercy seat, and from between the two cherubim, I will speak with you" (Ex. 25:10-22).

The Ark served as a symbol of the presence of Yahweh with his people. It was not worshipped but it served to remind the people of the Lord their God and of the worship and service he required. The sculpted icon of the cherubim fulfilled a liturgical ministry. Before the Incarnation, all artistic expression of the heavenly is limited to the angelic world due to the fear of idolatry. (See note at the end of the chapter.)

Thus, while the Old Testament proclaims the invisible, holy, and transcendentally glorious reality of Yahweh, who alone is true God, and while it condemns all idolatry, it also without any hesitation proclaims the right use of created matter in the worship and service of God. Further, it does assert (in the early chapters of Genesis) that man, as male and female, is made in the image and after the likeness of God (e.g., 1:26). Man is *not* the image but is made *in* the image. Such an assertion leaves open the question as to who is *the* image! We have to wait for the Incarnation to know, as the New Testament teaches, that the Son of God, the Word made flesh, is the one and only Image of the Father. And in this knowledge we also know that the purpose of the Incarnation is to conform those who are made *in* the image to *the* Image, to become like him (Rom. 8:9; I Cor. 15:49; II Cor. 3:18; Eph. 4:24; Col. 3:10ff.).

What neither the Old nor New Testaments specifically address is whether or not it is admissible to make icons of the Incarnate Son or of those who bear his image and likeness (his Mother and the Saints). The Old Testament does, however, legitimate the use of material symbols as aids to the pure worship of Yahweh in spirit and in truth. Naturally, the iconodules made much of this in their appeal to the Bible.

FOR FURTHER READING

In all the major Bible Dictionaries there are articles on "Yahweh," "Idolatry," "Image(s)," and "Worship." Likewise, in the major books on the theology and religion of the Old Testament the subject of idolatry is treated. Philip E. Hughes, *The True Image: The Origin and Destiny of Man in Christ* (Grand Rapids: Eerdmanns, 1989) is filled with stimulating thoughts. Walter Kasper, *The God of Jesus Christ* (New York: Crossroad, 1984) is also very stimulating. There are chapters on the portrayal of YHWH in the Old and New Testaments in Peter Toon, *Our Triune God* (Wheaton: Victor Books, 1996).

Note

In the Orthodox Church the icons of Christ's resurrection develop the symbolism of the Ark. On a slab, representing the empty tomb and the lid of the Ark, is the abandoned winding sheet; and, on the ends of the slab, two cherubim stand facing the women who bear myrrh. Thus the "throne of mercy" reveals in Christ its real meaning. Via the icon, Yahweh appears on the "throne of mercy" and speaks from it.

On Orthodox Sunday, the feast of the icon, two passages from the Gospels, which speak of angels, are read—Matthew 18:10 and John 1:51. They are seen as teaching that (i) the many-eyed angels possess the gift of contemplating the Divine Light, and (ii) that after the Incarnation Christians receive this angelic gift expressed so powerfully by the icon.

CHAPTER ELEVEN

Iconoclasm Rejected

Not a single one of the writings of the iconoclasts has been preserved in its original form. We only know of the content of this literature where it has been preserved as part of the reply of the iconodules. Likewise, since the iconoclasts destroyed images wherever they found them, there have been preserved few examples of icons in churches and monasteries from the period of the controversy.

IN COMMON

Those who destroyed, and those who made and preserved Christian representational art, had much in common—commitment to the dogma of the Trinity, acceptance of the authority and the inspiration of the Holy Scriptures, and belief in the divine right of kings (emperors), for example. Also, with specific reference to images, both sides were in agreement over some basic principles and uses.

Each, for example, accepted that material objects can be a contact point between the praying man and the merciful God.

The iconoclasts restricted this materiality to the bread and wine of the Eucharist, the water of Baptism, the oil of Chrismation and the wood of the cross. In contrast, the iconodules included the whole of sanctified, representational art.

Then, also, each side was concerned about the large numbers of illiterate and unsophisticated members of the Church and their instruction in the holy Faith. All knew the power of art to inform the devotion of the people. For the iconodules representational art served as a holy book for the illiterate, for it proclaimed the Gospel message in pictures. For the iconoclasts, who remembered the use of such art in paganism and who heard the denunciation of Islam against all images, the pictures proclaimed a false message concerning the true identity of the Lord Jesus Christ, his Mother and the Saints. They reintroduced paganism and idolatry!

Further, each side proclaimed that Jesus Christ is the Image of God and that man is made in the image of God (Gen. 1:27). All were committed to this doctrine even though they made opposing deductions and applications from it in terms of the pictorial representation of Jesus Christ.

Finally, each side appealed to the Fathers and thus to antiquity. And, as we would expect, each side found evidence for its cause. During the first three or four centuries, Christianity was a minority Faith in an Empire where polytheism was the norm and where images/idols of the deities were worshipped. In this context, Christian writers condemned idolatry, citing the Scriptures of the Old Testament. Not unexpectedly, there was little representational art produced by Christians! However, when Christianity became an official, and then *the* official, religion of the Empire, the way was open, with the defeat of paganism, to develop Christian representational art, and to distinguish icons of Christ and the Saints from idols of the gods and goddesses of the defeated paganism. In this new art, the prohibition against any representation of the invisible, ineffable God (Yahweh, the Father) was constant.

THE COUNCIL OF HIERIA

The Emperor Leo III, the Isaurian, began a campaign against the cult of icons in 726. His son, Constantine V, who became Emperor in 741, also led a campaign to remove and destroy icons as well as to paint over art on church walls. Crosses, however, were allowed to remain. These Emperors, and also their successors, were of Semitic rather than Hellenic background. Their tradition did not have within it the cultic importance of the image. Further, they were engaged in war with Islam, which destroyed all images in its path. Thus, they were obviously aware of and sensitive to the charges made by Muslims about the supposed idolatry of Christians, who, it was said, worshipped icons.

The theological sympathies of Constantine V were more with the Monophysites than the Chalcedonians and he actually published under his own name a doctrinal statement on behalf of iconoclasm. Insisting that the *prosopon* of Christ is made up of both divine and human elements, he opposed representational art because it only presented the human nature. Thereby, he said, it severed that nature from his divine nature and negated the unity of Christ as one hypostasis and one nature. Thus an icon is a false image of Christ, who being both God and Man cannot be presented in an art form because Godhead by its very nature cannot be circumscribed. The only true image of Christ is that which he instituted—the sacramental Bread and Wine, his Body and Blood of the Holy Eucharist.

To press his doctrine and policy upon the Church and Empire, Constantine V called a Church Council which met in the Palace of Hieria, north of Chalcedon, from February to August 754. The Epitome of the Definition of this Iconoclastic Council was agreed by the Bishops in August, 754. It begins its theological claims in these words: "Satan misguided men, so that they worshipped the creature instead of the Creator. The Mosaic Law and the Prophets cooperated to undo this ruin; but in order to save mankind thoroughly, God sent his own Son, who turned us away from error and the worshipping of idols, and taught us the worshipping of God in spirit and in truth."

Against this background the Statement continues: "We [the 338 members] found that the unlawful art of painting living creatures blasphemed the fundamental doctrine of our salvation— namely, the Incarnation of Christ—and it contradicted the six holy synods [i.e., Ecumenical Councils]." The truth of the matter is that Jesus Christ is One Person, God made Man, and consequently, an icon of Christ is an image of God and Man. Thus in his foolish mind, the painter, in his representation of the flesh of Jesus, has depicted the Godhead which cannot be represented. He has mingled what cannot be mingled. Therefore, he is guilty of a double blasphemy—making an image of the Godhead and mingling the Godhead and the manhood. Further, anyone who uses the icon is also guilty of blasphemy.

In terms of Christology, the Council taught that the manhood of Christ, being the humanity of the Logos, was completely assumed by the divine nature and totally deified.

> For it should be considered that the flesh [of Jesus] was also the flesh of God the Word, without any separation, perfectly assumed by the divine nature and made wholly divine. How could it now be separated and represented apart? So is it with the human soul of Christ which mediates between the Godhead of the Son and the dulness [thickness] of the flesh. As the human flesh is at the same time flesh of God the Word, so is the human soul also soul of God the Word, and both at the same time, the soul being deified as well as the body, and the Godhead remaining undivided even in the separation of the soul from the body in his voluntary passion. For where the soul of Christ is there is his Godhead; and where the body of Christ is there is his Godhead. (Percival, *Seven Councils*, p. 544.)

Here are echoes of the Definition of the Council of Chalcedon ("without any separation") and of the two wills and energies of the Council of Constantinople III, but the theory of *communicatio idiomatum* is pushed to an extreme limit. Thereby, the real humanity and manhood of Christ is minimized and deification is exaggerated.

The Statement goes on to claim, as the Emperor had done, that "the only admissible figure of the humanity of Christ is bread and wine in the holy Supper. This and no other form, this and no other type, has he chosen to represent his Incarnation."

And then, with reference to representational art depicting the Saints, the Epitome states:

> Christianity has rejected the whole of heathenism, and so not merely heathen sacrifices, but also the heathen worship of images. The Saints live on eternally with God, although they have died. If anyone thinks to call them back again to life by a dead art, discovered by the heathen, he makes himself guilty of blasphemy. Who dares attempt with heathenish art to paint the Mother of God, who is exalted above all heavens and the Saints? It is not permitted to Christians, who have the hope of the resurrection, to imitate the customs of demon-worshippers, and to insult the Saints, who shine in so great glory, by common dead matter. (*Ibid.*, p. 544.)

In short, God has forbidden the making of graven images in the Ten Commandments and this prohibition remains in force!

Next, it forbids the production and demands the destruction of "every likeness which is made out of any material and color whatever by the evil art of painters." Then a series of anathemas are declared among which are the following concerning icons of Christ:

8. If anyone ventures to represent the divine image (*charakter*) of the Word after the Incarnation with material colors, let him be anathema!
9. If anyone ventures to represent in human figures, by means of material colors, by reason of the Incarna-

tion, the Substance or Person of the Word, which cannot be depicted, and does not rather confess that even after the Incarnation he, the Word, cannot be depicted, let him be anathema!

13. If anyone represents in a picture the flesh deified by its union with the Word, and thus separates it from the Godhead, let him be anathema!

Then with respect to Mary, *Theotokos*, and the Saints, are the following anathemas:

15. If anyone shall not confess the holy ever-virgin Mary, truly and properly the Mother of God, to be higher than every creature whether visible or invisible, and does not with sincere faith seek her intercessions as one having confidence in her access to our God, since she bare him, let him be anathema.

16. If anyone shall endeavor to represent the forms of the Saints in lifeless pictures with material colors which are of no value (for this notion is vain and introduced by the devil), and does not rather represent their virtues as living images in himself, let him be anathema.

17. If anyone denies the profit of the invocation of Saints, let him be anathema. (*Ibid.*, pp. 545-46.)

These make clear that the Eastern Christian Iconoclasts were not like Western Protestants of a later time since the former, unlike the latter, regarded the intercession of the Saints as an important part of the Faith.

ANATHEMAS AT THE COUNCIL OF NICEA (787)

At the beginning of what eventually was recognized as the Seventh Ecumenical Council, certain bishops who had supported the cause of iconoclasm confessed their sin and error, asking to

172

be received back into the communion of the Catholic Church. These confessions indicate both what was central to the iconoclasts and to the iconodules.

Bishop Basil of Ancyra confessed his faith in the Holy Trinity and proceeded:

> I ask for the intercessions of our spotless Lady the Holy Mother of God, and those of the heavenly powers and those of all the saints. And receiving their holy and honorable relics with all honor, I salute and venerate these with honor, hoping to have a share in their holiness. Likewise also the venerable icons of the incarnation of our Lord Jesus Christ, in the humanity he assumed for our salvation; and of our spotless Lady, the holy Mother of God; and the angels like unto God; and of the holy Apostles, Prophets, Martyrs, and of all the Saints—the sacred icons of all these I salute and venerate. (*Ibid.*, p. 533.)

Among his anathemas were these:

> Anathema to the calumniators of the Christians, that is to the icon breakers.

> Anathema to those who apply the words of Holy Scripture, which were spoken against idols, to the venerable images.

> Anathema to those who do not salute the holy and venerable icons.

> Anathema to those who say that Christians have recourse to the icons as to gods.

> Anathema to those who call the sacred icons idols.

> Anathema to those who say that the making of images is a diabolical invention and not a tradition of our holy Fathers. (*Ibid.*, p. 534.)

173

As we would expect, what these anathemas condemn is that which the Emperor Constantine V and the Council of Hieria had approved.

The official anathemas of the Council of Nicea II were brief and to the point, making very clear what was the error and the sin of iconoclasm and what was the essence of iconodulism.

If anyone does not confess that Christ our God can be represented in his humanity, let him be anathema.

If anyone does not accept representation in art of evangelical scenes, let him be anathema.

If anyone does not salute such representations as standing for the Lord and his Saints, let him be anathema.

If anyone rejects any written or unwritten traditions of the Church, let him be anathema.

Eventually iconoclasm fell, and when this occurred it fell like Lucifer, never to rise again in the Catholic Church of the East.

IN SUMMARY

In his fascinating book, *The Art of the Icon* (1990), Paul Evdokimov provides a good summary of the nature of Iconoclasm and writes:

For the iconoclasts, every image could only be a portrait, and of course a portrait of God was inconceivable. Their exclusively realistic conception of art drove them to deny any symbolic character to the icon. From the sacramental perspective, they believed quite correctly in symbols, that is in the real presence of the symbolized thing or person in its symbol, but they denied any presence of the person represented, the prototype, in his iconographic image. Once this conception was accepted, the icon fell into the category of profane art, since it was obviously not a sacrament. From their point of view, the claim that icons were a sacred art simply clothed them in superstition and even heresy. It was therefore necessary to choose between a photographic likeness, as we would say today, and a symbolic likeness. The two were mutually exclusive. The iconoclasts could only conceive of an art that was realistic and reproduced the visible of the visible, thus making a copy of the visible. They could not see that the icon portrayed the "visible of the invisible," and the invisible *in* the visible.

And he continues:

> The only adequate image of Christ was, therefore, the Eucharist because it was consubstantial (*homoousios*) and identical (*tauto*) with him in nature (*kat'ousian*). Now the Eucharist is a miracle in which the cosmic matter of bread and wine are changed into the heavenly matter of the transfigured body of Christ. But the miracle of the *metabole*, or transformation, takes place without producing any likeness or resemblance....The visible bread is simply stated to be identical with the invisible heavenly body, but the operation gives no place to any visual manifestation. The Eucharist cannot in any way be an icon for it is uniquely the Lord's Supper which must be *consumed* and not *contemplated* (pp. 193-95).

It is obvious that the iconoclasts and the iconodules were unable to agree because their whole foundation of thinking was different. They were working from different theological and philosophical principles.

FOR FURTHER READING

For the texts used in this chapter see Percival's edition of the Seven Councils. Pelikan, *The Spirit of Eastern Christendom,* and Meyendorff, *Christ in Eastern Thought,* and Davis, *The First Seven Ecumenical Councils,* also have useful material on iconoclasm as well as suggestions for further reading.

CHAPTER TWELVE

Orthopraxis Explained—
Veneration of Icons

The connection between the dogma of the first six Ecumenical Councils and that of Nicea II is the Incarnation. Because the eternal Son became Man, the Holy Trinity of the Father, the Son and the Holy Spirit was revealed. In, by and through the Son we know the Holy Triad. Further, because of the Incarnation, the veneration of icons is rendered both valid and good. Since the Son of God took flesh and dwelt among us, the invisible became visible and thus, it was possible to depict him by representational art. The Council of Nicea (787) upheld the veneration of icons as an inevitable result of the Incarnation. The Son is the Icon of the Father.

FROM 692 TO 787

The veneration of icons was not a new development in the eighth century when iconoclasm waged war on iconodulism. In fact, there are two canons of the Quinisext Council (692) which illuminate the situation concerning veneration of images/icons in the Greek-speaking churches before the rise of iconoclasm.

First of all, Canon 73 speaks of the veneration of the Cross:

> Since the life-giving cross has shown to us salvation, we should be careful that we render due honor to that by which we were saved from the ancient fall. Wherefore, in mind, in word, in feeling giving veneration (*proskunesis*) to it, we command that the figure of the cross, which some have placed on the floor, be entirely removed therefrom, lest the trophy of the victory won for us be desecrated by the trampling under foot of those who walk over it. Therefore those who from this present represent on the pavement the sign of the cross, we decree are to be excommunicated.

Veneration of the Cross is by the mind and heart, through words and action and with the senses (bowings, kisses etc.).

In the second place, Canon 82 speaks of the veneration of icons.

> In some pictures of the venerable icons, a lamb is painted to which the Precursor points his finger, which is received as a type of grace, indicating beforehand through the Law, our true Lamb, Christ our God. Embracing, therefore, the ancient types and shadows as symbols of the truth, and patterns given to the Church, we prefer "grace and truth," receiving it as the fulfillment of the Law. In order, therefore, that "that which is perfect" may be delineated to the eyes of all, at least in colored expression, we decree that the figure in human form of the Lamb who taketh away the sin of the world, Christ our God, be henceforth exhibited in images, instead of the ancient lamb, so that all may understand by means of it the depth of the humiliation of the Word of God, and that we may recall to our memory his conversation in the flesh, his passion and salutary death, and his redemption which

was wrought for the whole world. (Percival, *Seven Councils,* pp. 398, 401.*)*

Commenting on this Canon, John Meyendorff wrote:

> The negative attitude of the Quinisext Council towards symbolism, and its emphasis upon the concrete and historical reality of the incarnation as the authentic foundation of the art of images, made it inevitable that the debate started by the iconoclastic decree of Emperor Leo III should immediately become a Christological debate; the problem was already posed within the framework of a theology of the incarnation. (Meyendorff, *Christ in Eastern Thought,* p. 178.)

Germanus, Patriarch of Constantinople under Leo III, had a clear view of the relation of icons to Jesus Christ.

> In eternal memory of the life in the flesh of our Lord Jesus Christ, of his passion, his saving death and the redemption of the world, which result from them, we have received the tradition of representing him in his human form, i.e., in his visible theophany, understanding that in this way we exalt the humiliation of God the Word (Cited by Meyendorff, *Ibid.,* p. 178).

Thus, an icon is not an image of the incomprehensible and immortal Godhead, but of the human character of the incarnate Word and Son.

Also, during the reign of Leo III another, and now justly famous, defense of iconodulism was made. In his monastery of St. Sabbas in Palestine and under Arab rule, John of Damascus wrote his *On the Divine Images: Three Apologies Against Those Who Attack the Divine Images.* St. John had no doubt that we are "to use all our senses to produce worthy images of Christ, and we sanctify the noblest of the senses, which is that of sight. For just as words edify the ear, so also the image stimulates the eye. What the book is to the literate, the image is to the illiterate. Just as words speak to the ear, so the image speaks to the sight; it brings us understanding" (I.17).

Icons are not only permissible but right and good because of the Incarnation, claimed St. John, who also explained:

> In former times, God who is without form or body, could never be depicted. But now when God is seen in the flesh conversing with men, I make an image of the God whom I see. I do not worship matter; I worship the Creator of matter who became matter for my sake, who willed to take his abode in the flesh; who worked out my salvation through matter. Never will I cease honoring the matter which wrought my salvation! I honor it, but not as God. (I.16)

Later, St. John provided a definition of an image.

> An image is a likeness, or a model, or a figure of something, showing in itself what it depicts. An image is not always like its prototype in every way. For the image is one thing, and the thing depicted is another; one can always notice differences between them, since one is not the other, and vice versa. I offer the following example: An image of a man, even if it is a likeness of his bodily form, cannot contain his mental powers. It has no life; it cannot think, or speak, or hear, or move. A son is the natural image of his father, yet is different from him, for he is a son and not a father.

Thus, he rejected the argument of the iconoclasts that an image is of the same essence as its prototype.

St. John also provided an explanation of the nature of worship. First and foremost, there is absolute worship which is adoration, reverence, thankfulness and confession offered to God, and to God alone. That is to the God and Father of our Lord Jesus Christ, the very God from whom proceeds the Holy Spirit. He is the source of all glory, all goodness, unapproachable light, incomparable sweetness, boundless perfection and who alone as the Blessed, Holy and Undivided Trinity is worthy to be adored, worshipped, glorified and desired.

In the second place, there is worship in a relative sense (= veneration). For example, when God rests in holy persons, who by grace have become likenesses of himself, then these persons (e.g., the *Theotokos* and the Saints) may be offered relative worship. As St. John put it: "Since they are truly gods, not by nature, but because they partake of the divine nature, they are to be venerated, not because they deserve it on their own account, but because they bear in themselves him who is by nature worshipful" (III. 33).

Also holy objects may be venerated—e.g., the holy sites in Jerusalem, Judea and Galilee, relics, the book of the Gospels, the Emperor and, of course, icons. "We venerate images: it is not veneration offered to matter, but to those who are portrayed through matter in the images. And any honor given to an image is transferred to its prototype" (III. 41).

NICEA (787)

Those who embraced iconodulism were those who of necessity held that the Son of God truly and really became man, a real man. They set aside not merely Docetism, but also all types of Monophysitism. Thus, when the Bishops made their declaration concerning icons at the Ecumenical Council of 787 they began with a strong affirmation of the reality of Jesus depicted in the Gospels:

> **To make our confession short we declare that we keep unchanged all the ecclesiastical traditions handed down to us, whether in writing or verbally, one of which is the making of pictorial representations, agreeable to the history of the preaching of the Gospel: a tradition useful in**

many respects, but especially in this, that so the Incarnation of the Word of God is shown forth as real and not merely imaginary, and brings us a similar benefit. For, things that mutually illustrate one another undoubtedly possess one another's message.

Then the Bishops made it abundantly clear that, while they agreed with iconoclasts in venerating the sacred cross, they also firmly believed in the production of representational art to depict Jesus Christ, the *Theotokos*, the Saints and the Angels.

We, therefore, following the royal pathway and the divinely inspired authority of our holy Fathers and the traditions of the Catholic Church (for, as we all know, the Holy Spirit indwells her), define with full precision and accuracy that just as the figure of the precious and lifegiving Cross, so also the venerable and holy pictures (*eikonas*), as well in painting and mosaic as in other fit materials, should be set forth in the holy churches of God, and on the sacred vessels and on the vestments and on the hangings and in the pictures *(sanisin)* both in houses and by the wayside, namely, the picture *(eikon)* of our Lord and Savior Jesus Christ, of our spotless Lady *(despoines)* the holy Mother of God *(theotokos)*, of the honorable angels, of all holy and pious men.

The purpose of such art is to lead the faithful forward in the path of deification/divinization as they are reminded of the Prototypes represented on the icon. In this context, it is appropriate that veneration be offered to the image and thus through the image veneration be given to the prototype.

For the more frequently they are seen in artistic representation the more readily are men lifted up to the memory of, and the longing after, their prototypes; and to these should be given salutation and honorable rever-

ence *(aspasmon kai timetiken proskunesin)*, not indeed the true worship *(latreiav)* which is fitting *(prepei)* for the Divine nature alone; but to these, as to the figure *(tupo)* of the holy and life-giving Cross, and to the holy Gospels, and to the other sacred objects, incense and lights may be offered according to ancient pious custom. For the honor which is paid to the picture *(eikon)* passes on to that which the picture represents, and he who reveres *(proskunon)* the picture reveres in it the subject represented.

It is important to note that the word used to denote the veneration of relative worship offered to the icons is *proskunesis*, which was used of the honor and reverence paid to the memorials and portraits of the Emperor.

So it is that the teaching of our holy Fathers, that is, the Tradition of the Catholic Church, which from one end of the earth to the other has received the Gospel, is strengthened. And so it is that we follow Paul, who spoke in Christ, and the entire, divine apostolic company and the holy fathers, holding fast the traditions which we have received. So we sing prophetically the triumphal hymns of the Church: "Rejoice greatly, O daughter of Zion; shout, O daughter of Jerusalem: rejoice and be glad with all thine heart. The Lord hath taken away from thee the oppression of thine enemies. The Lord is a King in the midst of thee; thou shalt not see evil any more, and peace shall be unto thee for ever [Zeph. 3:14-15, Septuagint]."

Those, therefore, who dare to think or teach otherwise, or who follow the wicked heretics to spurn the traditions of the Church and to invent some novelty, or who reject some of those things which the Church has received (e.g., the Book of the Gospels, or the image of the Cross, or the pictorial icons, or the holy relics of a martyr), or who devise perverted and evil prejudices against cherishing

the lawful traditions of the Catholic Church, or who turn to common uses the sacred vessels of the venerable monasteries, we command that they be deposed if they be Bishops or Clerics and excommunicated if they be monks or lay people.

Then come the anathemas against iconoclasm which are printed in chapter eleven above.

The content of this decree concerning images/icons may be summarized by saying the following:

1. The offering of adoration (*latreia*) to any created person or thing is idolatry and is forbidden by God.
2. The sacred pictures, the icons, are to be given veneration (*proskunesis*) according to holy tradition.
3. The icons are useful for instruction in the Faith.
4. The icons are required to preserve the truth that Jesus Christ is a real Person with true manhood and he was not merely a fantasy, theory or idea.
5. The veneration given to the icon passes on to the person, human or angelic, whom the icon represents.
6. The Lord Jesus Christ is truly God and truly Man. In his Godhead he is uncircumscribed, but in his Manhood he is limited and thus may be portrayed in painting, mosaic or other suitable materials.

The translator, Dr. Henry R. Percival, to whom we are all greatly indebted for his work on the Seven Councils, makes the following comments in his introduction to his translation of the Decree of Nicea (787):

> The Council decreed that similar veneration and honor should be paid to the representations of the Lord and of the Saints as was accustomed to be paid to the "laurata" and tablets representing the Christian emperors, to wit, that they should be bowed to, and saluted with kisses, and attended with lights

and the offering of incense. But the Council was most explicit in declaring that this was merely a veneration of honor and affection, such as can be given to the creature, and that under no circumstances could the adoration of divine worship be given to them but to God alone. (Percival, *Seven Councils*, p. 526.)

Then, to make the distinction between veneration and worship as clear as possible, Dr. Percival added:

The Greek language has in this respect a great advantage over the Hebrew, the Latin and the English; it has a word which is a general word and is properly used of the affectionate regard and veneration shown to any person or thing, whether to the divine Creator or to any of his creatures, this word is *proskunesis*; it has also another word which can properly be used to denote only the worship due to the most high God, this word is *latreia*. When then the Council defined that the worship of "latria" was never to be given to any but God alone, it cut off all possibility for ido*latry*, mario*latry*, icono*latry*, or any other *latry*, except theo*latry*. If, therefore, any of these other "latries" exist or have existed, they exist or have existed not in accordance with, but in defiance of, the decree of the Second Council of Nicea. (*Ibid.*, pp. 526-27.)

In the light of the lack of exact, equivalent terms for *proskunesis* and *latreia* in Latin and English it is not perhaps surprising that the Decree of this Council has been both badly translated and greatly misunderstood in the West. The simplest way to state the relation of *proskunesis* and *latreia* is to picture two circles which have the same center, with the larger (*proskunesis*) including the smaller (*latreia*).

IN SUMMARY

The nature of the icon is very different from that of the Bread and Wine of the Eucharist. Again Paul Evdokimov in *The Art of the Icon* (1990), provides an explanation which is helpful:

> The icon finds its place on a totally different level and thus escapes any charge of idolatry. The very word *icon* (from the word *eiko* and meaning *likeness, similitude*) suppresses any identification and underlines the *difference in nature* between the image and its prototype, "between the representation and what is represented." We can never say that "the icon is Christ" as we say that "this bread is the body of Christ." This would obviously be idolatry. The icon is an image which witnesses to a presence in a very specific way: it allows a prayerful communion with the glorified nature of Christ; it is, however, not a eucharistic communion, that is, substantial. It is rather a spiritual communion, a mystical communion with the Person of Christ.

And he continues:

> The icon brings about a meeting *in prayer*, without localizing this communion in the icon as a material object. The meeting nonetheless takes place through and with the icon as a vehicle of the presence. In an icon, the *Hypostasis*, Christ's person, "enhypostasizes" not a substance (wood and colors) but the *likeness*. It is the likeness alone and not the board that is the meeting place where we encounter the presence.

Further, he makes clear the importance of focusing on the "likeness:"

> This likeness is fundamental to an understanding of the real nature of the icon. It is tied solely to the contemplation of

186

the Church. This is how, in truth, the Church sees Christ *liturgically*... The mystery of the icon resides in this dynamic and mysterious likeness with the prototype, with the whole Christ, a likeness attested by the Church. (*Ibid.*, pp. 195-96.)

Finally, connecting all this with the doctrine of the *enhypostasis* developed by Leontius (see chap. 9, p. 146 above) and accepted in the Orthodox Church, Evdokimov states:

The notion of *enhypostatos* is at the base of the Fathers' doctrine. It explains how, through the image, we can invoke the presence of its prototype. (*Ibid.*, p. 198.)

FOR FURTHER READING

The documents relating to the Council in Percival, *Seven Councils,* are invaluable; Meyendorff's book, *Christ in Eastern Thought,* is of great help, as is also Leo D. Davis's historical account in *The First Seven Ecumenical Councils*. Finally, see St. John of Damascus, *On the Divine Images*, trans. David Anderson (Crestwood, NY: St. Valdimir's Seminary Press, 1980).

Epilogue

Jesus Christ is the same yesterday and today and forever declares the writer of the Letter to the Hebrews (13:8). This is the glorious truth of Christianity. In God's economy, Jesus Christ is always the same: he does not change! *Yesterday*, while on earth as the Incarnate Son, Jesus "in the days of his flesh offered up prayers and supplications with loud cries and tears unto him [the Father] who was able to save him from death" (5:7). *Today* he represents his people in the presence of the Father as the high priest who is able to sympathize with them in their weakness, because "in every respect he has been tempted as we are, yet without sin" (4:15). *Forever* he lives "to make intercession for them" (7:25) to the Father in heaven.

It is the truth concerning this Jesus Christ, now exalted in heaven as the great high priest, which is declared by the Ecumenical Councils. For Jesus to be the same yesterday, today and forever in the dynamic meaning of the Letter to the Hebrews, he also had to be (as Heb. 1-2 makes clear) the eternal, unchanging Son of the Father. Before all ages and through all ages and unto all ages he is the only-begotten Son of the Father. As the Word and the Son of the Father he will not change! Yet, without ceasing to be who he was and is, he did take to himself human nature in the womb of Mary, the *Theotokos*.

Thus, in both an economic sense (Heb. 13:8) and an ontological sense (orthodox dogma) he is truly the same yesterday, today and forever. The truth set forth in Scripture and the truth set forth in the doctrinal decrees of the Councils is one truth, expressed in two complementary forms. And the Church needs both forms!

This one Truth is the common possession of all Christians for all space and time until Jesus by his Parousia and Second Coming truly declares to the whole cosmos that he is the Lord and also that he is the same yesterday, today and forever.

For the traditional Orthodox or Roman Catholic the decrees of the Seven Councils are received as holy Tradition, which cannot be changed, only further expanded. There may be some debate as to the precise meaning of the dogma, but its authority as Church teaching is not in doubt. This being so, it is the constant prayer of many that the world will witness a continued, expanding, informed and joyous commitment to the doctrinal decrees of these Councils and to their implications for worship and evangelism, by Bishops, theologians, clergy and people, of both the Orthodox and Roman Catholic Churches. This enlarging embrace and celebration of orthodoxy will, of course, necessarily mean the recognition and rejection of heresies, errors and false religion, which are as much a problem today as they were yesterday. (See Appendix I for details of error entering the Roman Catholic Church through inaccurate translations.) Further, we may suggest that such a dynamic and wholehearted recovery of holy dogma would have repercussions through the ecumenical movement upon Protestantism worldwide.

For traditional Protestants the authority of the dogma of the Councils is not so straightforward as it is for Catholics of the East and West. They are ready and enthusiastic to say that "Jesus Christ is the same yesterday, today and forever;" but they say that the teaching of the Councils is to be received only if and where it is in agreement with the content and intention of the

Holy Scriptures. So there has been a general readiness in the conservative Reformed and Lutheran traditions to accept the patristic doctrines of the Holy Trinity and of Christology because they are seen as either within or required by the Holy Scriptures, as they interpret them. However, there has been a general hesitancy in these traditions to call Mary the *Theotokos* and a definite refusal to follow the teaching of Nicea II on the veneration of icons.

Anglicanism, which learned to see itself as expressing an English form of Reformed Catholicism, began its modern existence in the sixteenth century during the reign of Henry VIII and his successors in England. It has always had a special respect for the teaching of the first four Ecumenical Councils (comparing and linking Four Councils to Four Gospels) and has also quietly accepted that of the Fifth and Sixth. But its attitude towards the decrees of the Seventh Council, Nicea II, has not been consistent, primarily because the teaching on the veneration of icons was originally interpreted through the excessive, western veneration (sometimes idolatry) of images (which Protestants of the sixteenth century strongly opposed). This attitude, with its sustained appeal to Scriptural texts, is most clearly seen in the iconoclast rhetoric and teaching of the lengthy homily, "Against Peril of Idolatry," in *The Second Book of Homilies* (1563), authorized by Queen Elizabeth for clergy to read in church instead of preaching a sermon.

To appreciate this position of the Church of England in the late sixteenth century, we must notice two authoritative statements from the Church on the General or Ecumenical Councils. First, the twenty-first Article of the doctrinal statement known as the *Thirty-Nine Articles of the Church of England* (1571) declares:

> General Councils may not (*non possunt*) be gathered together without the commandment and will of Princes. And when they be gathered together, (forasmuch as they be an assem-

bly of men, whereof all be not governed with the Spirit and the Word of God,) they may err, and sometimes have erred, even in things pertaining unto God. Wherefore things ordained by them as necessary to salvation have neither strength nor authority, unless it may be declared that they be taken out of Holy Scripture.

To set this statement in context, we must bear in mind that the Council of Trent was then in session and that this Roman Catholic Council, which was anti-Protestant, had been called into session not by Kings (Princes) but by the Pope alone! Further, Protestants knew about such councils as the "Robber Council" of 449.

In chapter XIV of the *Reformatio Legum Ecclesiasticarum* (1553), which replaced the books of medieval canon law in the Church of England, the mind of this Church is expressed in these terms:

Though we gladly give honor to the Councils, especially those that are General, we judge that they ought to be placed far below the dignity of canonical Scriptures: and we make a great distinction between the Councils themselves. For some of them, especially these four (the Council of Nicea, the first Council of Constantinople, and the Councils of Ephesus and Chalcedon) we embrace and receive with great reverence. And we bear the same judgment about many others held afterwards, in which we see and confess that the most holy fathers gave many weighty and holy decisions according to the Divine Scriptures, about the blessed and supreme Trinity, about Jesus Christ our Lord and Savior, and the redemption of man obtained through him. But we think that our faith ought not to be bound by them, except so far as they can be confirmed by Holy Scripture. For it is manifest that some Councils have sometimes erred, and defined contrary to one another, partly on actions of law and partly even of faith.

If Article XXI is read in the light of this explanation, then it is reasonably clear that the first four Councils, at least, are not included in the list of those which erred. Other sources (e.g., the homily "Against Peril of Idolatry") speak of a total of Six Ecumenical Councils being received as teaching the truth of the Faith. However, as we noted above, there has been ambivalence or confusion concerning the Seventh Council. Little was known of it in the West in the sixteenth and seventeenth centuries, and where it was known, it was known in a misleading translation—e.g., *proskunesis* was rendered by *adoratio*, which meant that the fine distinction of meaning in the Greek text between genuine worship (*latreia* = *adoration*) of God as God and veneration (*proskunesis*) of icons of Jesus, the Angels and the Saints was lost in the Latin text!

There is no official Statement of the Church of England or of the Anglican Communion of Churches, which explicitly states that the doctrinal decrees of Nicea II are to be accepted. Yet, since many Anglicans have used and do use icons (especially since the rise of the Anglo-Catholic movement in the mid-nineteenth century) in the spirit of the teaching of Nicea II, it is probably right to say that the Anglican Communion of Churches does not reject, and for all practical purposes accepts, the doctrinal teaching of the Seventh Ecumenical Council.

Of course, if Protestants in general and Anglicans in particular, were to receive the whole Faith which is presupposed, declared and explained in the decrees of the Seven Ecumenical Councils, this commitment would require adjustments or even major changes in their practical expression of Christianity today. Their Liturgies and forms of worship, their Spirituality, their Dogmatics (Systematic Theology), their evaluation of the Reformation of the sixteenth century, their doctrine and practice of the ordained ministry, their church discipline, and their reading and interpreting of the Bible would all be candidates for renewal.

A final thought—anyone who studies the Seven Councils and their decrees cannot avoid such questions as: Is there a way to the truth, concerning Who is God?, Who is Jesus?, and What is the Gospel?, as stated in a propositional and rational form, without long and bitter controversies? Is it possible to have Church dogma without first having painful and demanding debate? Now, if it be the case that the Church did actually arrive at Truth in her dogma of the Holy Trinity and the Person of Jesus Christ made known in two natures, then one must concede that Truth as addressed to the thinking mind (in contrast to Truth as presented in the common sense approach of the Gospels) requires debate for its clarification and final statement. Hopefully, that debate need not always be such as to make hearts bitter.

Further, in order for the Church to maintain in different centuries, places and languages the same dogma, there will need to be not only explanatory teaching to state what the received dogma is, but also debate to find the appropriate forms of its expression at any one time and place. And, since it seems that there are always people in the Church who revive discarded heresies—Arianism, Sabellianism, Unitarianism, Adoptionism, Nestorianism and Monophysitism—there will always also be need for controversy in order to defend the received dogma and to set aside alternative, erroneous forms of teaching. In other words, the Church will always need her servants who do for their generations what Athanasius, the Cappadocian Fathers and Leo the Great did for their own.

**Glory be to the Father, and to the Son,
and to the Holy Ghost;
As it was in the beginning, is now, and ever shall be,
world without end. *Amen***

Appendices
and
Bibliography

APPENDIX I

I Believe/We Believe

Prior to the year 325, all creeds were local in character. They were particularly associated with the preparation for baptism and the rite of baptism itself. From 325, a new custom developed of Bishops in synods producing creeds as tests of orthodoxy. Creeds for catechumens began with the words "I believe," while those produced by synods began with the words "We believe."

The most important examples of creeds as tests of orthodoxy are the Nicene Creed of 325, known as "the Creed of the 318 Fathers," and the Constantinopolitan Creed of 381, known as "the Creed of the 150 Fathers." Since the Middle Ages the latter has been called "the Nicene Creed," which is a little confusing since the Creed of 381 is not identical with that of 325.

After the Council of Constantinople produced its Creed, it was then used in the local churches of the East as a baptismal Creed. Thus it was used in the form, "I believe." In the latter part of the fifth century, this same Creed, still in the first person singular, was introduced into the Eucharist, first by the Monophysites (to emphasize their commitment to orthodoxy) and then by the Chalcedonians (or Catholics). Thus, it became a standard feature of the Divine Liturgy of the East.

Much later it was introduced into the Latin Liturgy of the West, where the usual Creed for Catechumens and Baptism was known as the Apostles' Creed. The Nicene Creed in the Liturgy began, as in the East, with the first person singular, "I believe" (*Credo*), and was in every way an honest translation, except that this Latin Creed had an extra phrase, *filioque* (= "and the Son"), which came after the words "who proceeds from the Father." Therefore, the Latin Nicene Creed contained the doctrine of the double procession of the Holy Spirit, "from the Father and the Son," in contrast to the single procession of the original Creed of Constantinople (381).

In English, the translation of the Latin Nicene Creed which has been most widely known since the sixteenth century is that found in the *Book of Common Prayer* (1549) of the Church of England.

I believe in one God the Father Almighty, Maker of heaven and earth, And of all things visible and invisible:

And in one Lord Jesus Christ, the only-begotten Son of God; Begotten of his Father before all worlds, God of God, Light of Light, Very God of very God; Begotten, not made; Being of one substance with the Father; By whom all things were made: Who for us men and for our salvation came down from heaven, And was incarnate by the Holy Ghost of the Virgin Mary, And was made man: And was crucified also for us under Pontius Pilate; He suffered and was buried: And the third day he rose again according to the Scriptures; And ascended into heaven, And sitteth on the right hand of the Father: And he shall come again, with glory, to judge both the quick and the dead; Whose kingdom shall have no end.

And I believe in the Holy Ghost, The Lord, and Giver of Life, Who proceedeth from the Father and the Son; Who with the Father and the Son together is worshipped and glorified; Who spake by the Prophets: And I believe one Catho-

lic and Apostolic Church: I acknowledge one Baptism for
the remission of sins: And I look for the Resurrection of the
dead: And the life of the world to come. *Amen.*

Somehow the "holy" as a description of the Church got left out
of this translation by Thomas Cranmer, Archbishop of Canterbury. Otherwise, it is a fairly literal translation of the Latin text
used in the Latin Mass of the later Middle Ages. The Latin
equivalent of the Greek, *homoousion to patri,* was
consubstantialem Patri, and is rendered "of one substance with
the Father." Another way of translating the phrase would have
been "consubstantial with the Father"—as became common in
later Roman Catholic translations.

Since the Second Vatican Council and the arrival on the ecclesiastical scene of new liturgies, there have come various attempts to introduce new translations of the "Nicene Creed"
into the liturgies for the Eucharist. The one which is found in
the modern Roman Catholic Mass, as well as in the new Prayer
Books of Anglican Churches, was produced by the Interna-
tional Committee on English Texts in the 1970s. It is as follows:

> We believe in one God, the Father, the Almighty, maker of
> heaven and earth, of all this is, seen and unseen.

> We believe in one Lord, Jesus Christ, the only Son of God,
> eternally begotten of the Father, God from God, Light from
> Light, true God from true God, begotten not made, of one
> Being with the Father. Through whom all things were made.
> For us and for our salvation he came down from heaven: by
> the power of the Holy Spirit he became incarnate from the
> Virgin Mary, and was made man. For our sake he was cruci-
> fied under Pontius Pilate; he suffered death and was buried.
> On the third day he rose again in accordance with the Scrip-
> tures; he ascended into heaven and is seated at the right hand

of the Father. He will come again in glory to judge the living and the dead, and his kingdom will have no end.

We believe in the Holy Spirit, the Lord, the giver of life, who proceeds from the Father and the Son. With the Father and the Son he is worshipped and glorified. He has spoken through the Prophets. We believe in one holy catholic and apostolic Church. We acknowledge one baptism for the forgiveness of sins. We look for the resurrection of the dead and the life of the world to come. *Amen.*

Obviously, this is a very different translation to that of the older Anglican Prayer Book and, importantly, the difference is not related to only changes in the use and meaning of the English language since the sixteenth century.

It appears that this modern translation was intended to introduce the possibility (or the reality) of revised dogma into the Church. The following are specific examples of this revisionism.

(i) As the Creed of the baptized faithful who meet to offer Thanksgiving in the Eucharist, the Creed should begin with the words, "I believe..." All the baptized together should say, "I believe...," for this Faith is the personal faith of each one! The use of "We believe..." is obviously contrary to the best Tradition, for it confuses a synodical Creed with a baptismal Creed.

Apparently, what lies behind the "we" is an attempt by modern liturgists to forge a "community" (a word which carries heavy secular overtones in American English) out of alienated individuals (i.e., modern people without roots). Thus, the Church is described as "the community of faithful individuals"; a sociological aim causes a change in the wording of the Creed of the holy Eucharist. The truth is that Christians come at God's call to the Eucharist as baptized believers; in the Creed they speak as particular persons, united in the Body of Christ in and by the Holy Spirit, as they each take full responsibility for their baptismal relation to the Father through the Son and in the Spirit.

The traditional use of "I" actually contains a meaning which we find hard to embrace living within the reality of modern individualism. The Church is one; she is a person, for she is the Bride of Christ. She is also our mother and teacher. Thus, to say "I believe..." is to accept that the Church corporately is the primary believer, and that each baptized believer is making the faith of the Church his own when reciting the Creed.[1]

(ii) In the first paragraph, which confesses faith in the Father as Creator, there is one major problem. The better translation is "visible and invisible." "Seen and unseen" is misguided, even mischievous. The word "invisible" suggests that it is impossible for the human eye to see the object in question (e.g., the seraphim). In contrast, the word "unseen" allows for that which is not now seen to be seen later under different conditions. It is interesting to note that modern biblical translations render *ta orata kai to aorata* (Colossians 1:15 and the exact words of the Creed) as "visible and invisible," not as "seen and unseen." Why did the translators of the Creed render the Greek words as "seen and unseen"? The probability is that the influence of the German Catholic theologian, Karl Rahner, caused the Committee to choose "seen and unseen." Behind these words lie his views on transcendentals, which are a not to be identified with the invisible world of angels and archangels. The intended meaning appears to be that what is now unseen will be seen as our mental and spiritual horizons enlarge!

(iii) In the second paragraph there are two major problems. First, instead of *homoousios* being translated, "one substance"

---

[1] The *Catechism of the Catholic Church* (1994) states in paragraph 167 that the Niceno-Constantinopolitan Creed (i.e., the Nicene Creed) is the Faith confessed by the bishops assembled in council (as in 381) "or more generally by the liturgical assembly of believers." This latter statement seems to open the door to justify the ICET "We believe..." translation.

or "consubstantial" [with the Father], the text has "of one Being" (where "Being" is capitalized). Again it appears that Rahner's influence was at work here. (It has been well said that Rahner and the other transcendental Thomists are "Aquikantists", attempting to square the circle by synthesizing St. Thomas with Immanuel Kant.) The doctrine of the Creed is that the Son possesses and shares the same, the identical, the numerically one Godhead or Deity with, the Father. Regrettably, the phrase, "of one Being," does not convey this foundational dogma with sufficient clarity for it allows for a generic unity (in contrast to a numerical unity) in the Godhead. Further, it may be read in the sense that the Father and the Son are one Being—that is, One God who has Two Names or Two Modes of Being. It is interesting to note that the English translations used in the various jurisdictions of the Orthodox Church usually have "one in essence" or "coessential" as the translation of *homoousios*.

Also, in the second paragraph there are the added words "by the power of," with reference to the virginal conception of Jesus by Mary. In neither the Greek nor the Latin text of the original Creed are any words to be found which could be translated "by the power of." They are an unlawful and deliberately misleading addition by the modern translators (who also made the same addition to the Apostles' Creed.) *Incarnatus est de Spiritu Sancto ex Maria Virgine et homo factus est* translates as "incarnate by the Holy Spirit of the Virgin Mary and was made man." Likewise, *kai sarkothenta ek Pneumatos Agiou kai Marias tes parthenou kai enanthropesanta* translates as "and was incarnate from the Holy Spirit and the Virgin Mary and became man."

Why did the Committee do it? Because, as their published Notes explain, some of their number wanted to make the conception of Jesus appear like the conception of Isaac and John the Baptist. The point of the Creed is, however, that the Word became the Word Incarnate by the Holy Spirit's unique presence and action in and upon the Virgin. All animals and all human beings are conceived by the power of the Holy Spirit, for he is present in Creation as the Creator; but only Jesus was uniquely conceived by the Holy Spirit, for he had no human father and was sent by the Father to be the New and Second Adam. The expression "the power of the Highest" in Luke 1:35 is a name of Yahweh, the LORD, and cannot be used (as is often done) to justify this addition to the text of the original Creed. In fact, to use this modern translation and know what is being stated is to embrace heresy—that the conception of Jesus was not unique, only remarkable! It is to suggest that he actually had a human father.

More recently, the tendency in modern liturgical circles has been to translate the Creed within the rubrics required by inclusive language. This also is the policy followed by the Jesuit scholars in *Decrees of the Ecumenical Councils* (ed. N. J. Tanner), where we have the phrases "for us humans" and "he became human and was crucified." However, when it comes to the *homoousios* the translation is "consubstantial with the Father" and, in reference to the conception of Jesus by Mary, "incarnate from the Holy Spirit and the Virgin Mary" (there is no "by the power of" the Holy Spirit!).

In summary, those who wish to be faithful to the Father, the Son and the Holy Ghost, to the Church their Mother and Teacher, and to the Orthodox Faith set forth in the ancient councils and by the Church in her authentic Liturgy (*lex orandi: lex credendi*) must recite the authentic Creed in an honest translation. That of Dr. J. N. D. Kelly, which we have used in this book, is such a translation of the original Creed. Regrettably the so-called Nicene Creed in the modern Roman and Anglican Liturgies is not truly the Creed of Constantinople (381). It is the Creed of post-Vatican II theological liberalism.

APPENDIX II

New Formula: Novel Doctrine

The formula "God: Father, Son and Holy Spirit" is being increasingly used by Christians of varying persuasions— liberal and conservative, traditional and modern, Protestant and Catholic. It occurs in a variety of written sources from liturgies, from catechisms to theological studies. For example, there are traces of it in the new *Catechism of the Catholic Church* (1994) where in paragraph 257 we read, "God is love: Father, Son and Holy Spirit" (cf. also paragraph 261).

As far as I know, there is no evidence for the use of this formula in official English statements of the Christian Faith before the 1960s; likewise, there is, as far as I can tell, little or no evidence for its use by theologians before the post-World War II period.

Therefore, the question arises as to whether or not it is an acceptable statement of Christian orthodoxy. Of course, it may be an acceptable statement of heterodoxy, but our concern is to ascertain if it conveys the truth of the dogma of the Blessed Holy and Undivided Trinity of the decrees of the Ecumenical Councils.

THE RECEIVED TRADITION

Throughout its long history the Church has used certain formulas in her naming of the Holy Trinity. These include:

> In the Name of the Father, and of the Son, and of the Holy Spirit.

> Glory be to the Father, and to the Son, and to the Holy Spirit as it was in the beginning, is now, and ever shall be, world without end. *Amen.*

> The Blessing of God Almighty, the Father, and the Son, and the Holy Spirit be upon you and remain with you forever.

In the decrees of the Seven Ecumenical Councils, the shortest and clearest statement of the dogma and doctrine of the Holy Trinity is the first anathema of the Fifth Council, that of Constantinople II (553).

> **If anyone does not confess one nature or substance, one power and authority, of the Father, the Son and the Holy Spirit, consubstantial Trinity, one Deity worshipped in three hypostases or persons, let him be anathema. For there is one God and Father, of whom are all things, and one Lord Jesus Christ, through whom are all things, and one Holy Spirit, in whom are all things.**

Here the first sentence is what the Fathers called "theology" proper—the dogma of the Holy Trinity, One *ousia* and three *hypostaseis*. The second sentence is the Trinity known in the economy—God-as-God-is-towards-us/the world. In the doctrine of the economic Trinity, God is always "the Father," the Father who has an Only-begotten Son and a Holy Spirit—the Father who is facing the world as Creator and Redeemer.

In the historic liturgies of the Church (e.g. those of St. Chrysostom, St. Basil, the Roman Rite from the late patristic era and Archbishop Cranmer [1549]), we find both the dogma of the Holy Trinity and the expression of the economy of the Trinity. The Eucharistic Prayer is addressed to the Father, through the Son and in the Spirit; the sacrifice of praise is offered by the assembly to the Father, through the Son and in the Spirit. Yet, alongside and inside the celebration of the economy of God, there are expressions of the dogma of the Trinity (e.g. in the Nicene Creed and the Prefaces of the Eucharistic Prayer, where the Son is said to be consubstantial with the Father).

A NEW TRADITION INTRODUCED

In modern times, the Episcopal Church in the USA has pioneered the new formula—"God: Father, Son and Holy Spirit"—in Liturgy and Catechism. Other Churches such as the Anglican Church of Canada followed its lead. Therefore, we shall study its appearance within authorized Episcopal sources.

The Episcopal Church liturgists, who in the 1960s and 1970s produced what became the authorized Prayer Book (1979), decided to create a new way of speaking of and/or addressing "God" as "Trinity" to accompany the traditional, received ones which we noted above. Students of liturgy and doctrine are first aware of this novel formula in the misleading translation of the ancient Greek evening hymn, *Phos Hilaron*, in the Rite I service of Evening Prayer (p. 64). Here we have the line, "We sing thy praises, O God: Father, Son and Holy Spirit." If we take the colon seriously, this suggests that the one God who is addressed merely has three names and/or three attributes, rather than three subsisting Persons. Further, since the praise is addressed to "thee" (singular), the impression given (perhaps through a faulty employment of Elizabethan English) is that a modalistic one God with three names or attributes is the object of the singing ("thy praise"). Anyone who reads the original

Greek could never come to such an impression and conclusion!

It is, however, in the Holy Eucharist that the new formula is most obviously encountered. In the Acclamation at the beginning of the Holy Eucharist are these sentences:

> *Celebrant:* Blessed be God: Father, Son and Holy Spirit.
> *People:* And blessed be his kingdom, now and for ever. *Amen.*

The Acclamation is in both Rite I and II, as well as in the three Ordination services for Deacon, Priest and Bishop. Thus it is deeply ingrained in the public services. Further, the novel formula is also used in the Catechism of the 1979 Book.

In the Catechism, in answer to the question "What [not *Who*] is the Trinity?" we are told that "The Trinity is one God: Father, Son and Holy Spirit" (p. 852). The word "what" points to the way in which the "one God" is known—in three names, as modes, expressions or attributes. The use of the word "who," by contrast, would have pointed to Persons, and therefore would have required the omission of the colon and the addition of definite articles.

What is wrong with this Acclamation? To answer this question we need to note the important Blessing on which it is based. It was an intentional rewriting of the Blessing from the beginning of the Liturgy of the Catechumens in the Divine Liturgy of the Orthodox Church. In the latter, the priest blesses the people as he holds the Book of the Gospels saying: "Blessed is the kingdom of the Father and the Son and the Holy Spirit, now, and ever, and unto ages of ages." This blessing recognizes that there is one divine kingdom, but that there are three divine Persons in the one Godhead. Thus, this kingdom is the kingdom of all Three. It is "their" kingdom.

The Episcopalian revision of the Orthodox Blessing first of all addresses a "God" who is neither specifically "the Father" (as in the New Testament) nor "the Godhead" (as in the traditional Western theology of Augustine and Aquinas). Instead, "God" is the Divine Being, the one Person, who has three names or attributes—"Father, Son and Holy Spirit." That is, God is One, but is a triad in the sense that he has three special names or three modes of expression. (It is worthy of note that since 1979 it has become common in parts of the ECUSA to change the three names/attributes to "Creator, Redeemer and Sanctifier," to avoid all male images.) Apparently this "God" is like a triangle or a three-leaf clover in that, while he is really One, he is both manifested and experienced as threefold. The force of the colon between "God" and "Father, Son and Holy Spirit" is to suggest the equivalency of what is at each side of the colon.

Since the response of the people in the Acclamation is, "And blessed be *his* kingdom...," where the pronoun, *his*, is obviously in the singular, then the meaning suggested/intended is that there is one "God"—the "God" who has the three names, attributes or expressions. If "Father, Son and Holy Spirit" are intended not merely to be names, but truly the Names of Three distinct Persons (Gk. *hypostases* and *prosopa*) as the Church has taught concerning the Trinity, then the pronoun should be "their." For the kingdom is the kingdom of the Three Persons— the Father, the Son of the Father, and the Holy Spirit of the Father. They are Three Persons who share the one, identical divine nature and Godhead.

IN CONCLUSION

We conclude that since this Formula is not a genuinely Christian Trinitarian statement, whether it occurs in official liturgies or in theological books. The formula seems to be closely related to the tendency in western theology from early times through to modern theology to think of God as a Person with three names. Historically, the formula belongs to the form of statement associated with the heresy of Sabellianism, a heresy which was often anathematized by the Seven Ecumenical Councils. Further, the Western Creed known as the *Quicunque Vult* (The Athanasian Creed) was produced in the fifth century to keep the Latin Church free of Sabellianism—i.e., free from the teaching that God is One as a simple rather than complex unity, who is experienced in three expressions, as fatherly, as in Jesus and as Spirit.

Further, in the 1960s and the 1970s, it was common in Anglican theological circles to speak of the one, personal God in terms of three Manifestations or Modes of Being. These were Primordial Being (= the Father), Expressive Being (= the Son) and Unitive Being (= the Holy Spirit). Thus Holy Being, it was said, had let itself be known in this threefold symbolism. It is very probable that such theological concepts influenced the creators of the new liturgies.

The late Dr. Mascall, in a piece entitled "Quicunque Vult? Anglican Unitarians," had this to say about the Blessed, Holy and Undivided Trinity:

> The Trinity is not primarily a doctrine, any more than the incarnation is primarily a doctrine. There is a doctrine *about* the Trinity, as there are doctrines about many other facts of existence, but, if Christianity is true, the Trinity is not a doctrine; the Trinity is God. And the fact that God *is* Trinity— that in a profound and mysterious way there are three divine Persons eternally united in one life of complete perfection and beatitude—is not a piece of gratuitous mystification, thrust by dictatorial clergymen down the throats of an unwilling and helpless laity, and therefore to be accepted, if at all, with reluctance and discontent. It is the secret of God's most intimate life and being, into which, in his infinite love and generosity, he has admitted us; and is therefore to be accepted with amazed and exultant gratitude. (*Whatever Happened to the Human Mind?*, pp. 117-18.)

The God whom the true Christian Church proclaims is the fundamentally triune God of the Father and the Son and the Holy

Spirit. It is not a unitarian God to whom the trinitarian character is attached as a kind of secondary, symbolic appendage.

[For more concerning the revised doctrines of the 1979 Book of Common Prayer see Peter Toon, *Proclaiming the Gospel in the Liturgy*, $11.95, published by the Prayer Book (1928) Society of the Episcopal Church, P. O. Box 35220, Philadelphia, PA 19128. 1-800-PBS-1928.]

APPENDIX III

The Council of Trent on Images

[Session 25. Translation from Percival, *Seven Councils*, p. 551. There is a modern translation in Tanner, *Decrees of the Seven Ecumenical Councils*, vol. II, pp. 774 ff.]

The holy synod enjoins on all bishops, and others sustaining the office and charge of teaching that, according to the usage of the Catholic and Apostolic Church received from the primitive times of the Christian religion, and according to the consent of the holy Fathers, and to the decrees of sacred councils, they especially instruct the faithful diligently touching the intercession and invocation of saints; the honor paid to relics; and the lawful use of images—teaching them, that the saints, who reign together with Christ, offer up their own prayers to God for men; that it is good and useful suppliantly to invoke them, and to resort to their prayers, aid and help, for obtaining benefits from God, through his Son, Jesus Christ our Lord, who alone is our Redeemer and Saviour; but that they think impiously, who deny that the saints, who enjoy eternal happiness in heaven, are to be invoked; or who assert either that they do not pray for men; or, that the invocation of them to pray for each of us, even in particular, is idolatry; or, that it is repugnant to the word of God, and is opposed to the honor of the *one Mediator between God and men, Christ Jesus,* or, that it is foolish to supplicate, orally or inwardly, those who reign in heaven.

Also, that the holy bodies of holy martyrs and of others now living with Christ, which were the living members of Christ, and *the temples of the Holy Ghost,* and which are by him to be raised unto eternal life, and to be glorified, are to be venerated by the faithful, through which [bodies] many benefits are bestowed by God on men; so that they who affirm that veneration and honor are not due to the relics of saints; or, that these, and other sacred monuments, are uselessly honored by the faithful; and that the places dedicated to the memories of the Saints are vainly visited for the purpose of obtaining their aid; are wholly to be condemned, as the Church has already long since condemned, and doth now also condemn them.

Moreover, that the images of Christ, of the Virgin Mother of God and of the other Saints, are to be had and retained particularly in temples, and that due honor and veneration are to be awarded them; not that any divinity or virtue is believed to be in them, on account of which they are to be worshipped; or that anything is to be asked of them; or that confidence is to be reposed in images, as was of old done by Gentiles, who placed their hope in idols; but because the honor which is shown unto them is referred to the prototypes which they represent; in such wise that by the images which we kiss, and before which we uncover the head, and prostrate ourselves, we adore Christ, and venerate the Saints, whose similitude they bear. And this, by the decrees of councils, and especially of the second Synod of Nicea, has been ordained against the opponents of images.

And the bishops shall carefully teach this; that, by means of the histories of the mysteries of our Redemption, depicted by paintings or other representations, the people are instructed, and strengthened in remembering, and continually reflecting on the articles of faith; as also that great profit is derived from all sacred images, not only because the people are thereby admonished of the benefits and gifts which have been bestowed upon them by Christ, but also because the miracles of God through the means of the Saints, and their salutary examples, are set before the eyes of the faithful; that so, for those things they may give God thanks; may order their own life and manners in imitation of the Saints; and may be excited to adore and love God, and to cultivate piety. But, if any one shall teach or think contrary to these decrees, let him be anathema.

And if any abuses have crept in amongst these holy and salutary observances, the holy synod earnestly desires that they be utterly abolished; in such wise that no images conducive to false doctrine, and furnishing occasion of dangerous error to the uneducated, be set up. And if at times, when it shall be expedient for the unlearned people, it happen that the histories and narratives of Holy Scripture are portrayed and represented; the people shall be taught, that not thereby is the Divinity represented, as though it could be perceived by the eyes of the body, or be depicted by colors or figures. Moreover, in the invocation of saints, the veneration of relics, and the sacred use of images, every superstition shall be removed, all filthy lucre be abolished, finally, all lasciviousness be avoided; in such wise that figures shall not be painted or adorned with a wantonness of beauty: nor shall men also pervert the celebration of the saints, and the visitation of relics, into revelings and drunkenness; as if festivals are celebrated to the honor of the saints by luxury and wantonness. Finally, let so great care and diligence be used by bishops touching these matters, as that there appear nothing disorderly, or unbecomingly or confusedly arranged, nothing profane, nothing indecorous; *since holiness becometh the house of God.*

And that these things may be the more faithfully observed, the holy synod ordains, that it be lawful for no one to place, or cause to be placed, any unusual image in any place, or church, howsoever exempted, except it shall have been approved of by the bishop: also, that no new miracles are to be admitted, or new relics received, unless the said bishop has taken cognizance and approved thereof; who, as soon as he has obtained some certain information in regard of these matters shall, after having taken advice with theologians, and other pious men, act therein as he shall judge to be agreeable to truth and piety. But if any doubtful, or difficult abuse is to be extirpated, or, in fine, if any more serious question shall arise touching these matters, the bishop, before he decides the controversy, shall await the sentence of the metropolitan and of the bishops of the same province, in a provincial council; yet so, that nothing new, or that has not previously been usual in the Church, shall be decreed, without the most holy Roman Pontiff having been first consulted.

Select Bibliography

Atyia, A. S. *History of Eastern Christianity*. Notre Dame, IN: Notre Dame University Press, 1968.

Attwater, Donald. *The Christian Churches of the East*. 2 vols. Milwaukee: Marquette University Press, 1947-48.

Bindley, T. H. *The Oecumenical Documents of the Faith*. London: Methuen & Co., 1950.

Bright, William. *Select Sermons of St. Leo the Great . . . with his Twenty-Eighth Epistle, called the Tome*. 2nd ed. London: J. Masters, 1886.

Chestnut, Robert C. *Three Monophysite Christologies: Severus of Antioch, Philoxenus of Mabbug and Jacob of Sarug*. Oxford: Oxford University Press, 1976.

Cochrane, C. N. *Christianity and Classical Culture*. Oxford: Oxford University Press, 1944.

Cross, F. L., and E. A. Livingstone, eds. *The Oxford Dictionary of the Christian Church*. 2d rev. ed. London and New York: Oxford University Press, 1983.

Davis, L. D. *The First Seven Ecumenical Councils (325-787)*. Wilmington, DE: Michael Glazier Inc., 1987.

Evdokimov, Paul. *The Art of the Icon*. Redondo Beach CA: Oakwood Publications, 1990.

Frend, W. H. C. *The Rise of Christianity*. London and Philadelphia: Fortress Press, 1984.

_____. *The Rise of the Monophysite Movement*. Cambridge: Cambridge University Press, 1972.

Grillmeier, Aloys. *Christ in Christian Tradition*. Atlanta, GA: John Knox Press, 1975.

Hanson, R. P. C. *The Search for the Christian Doctrine of God*. Edinburgh: T & T Clark, 1988.

Hardy, E. R. *Christology of the Later Fathers*. London and Philadelphia: Westminster Press, 1954.

Hughes, Philip E. *The True Image: The Origin and Destiny of Man in Christ*. Grand Rapids and Leicester: Eerdmanns, 1989.

John of Damascus. *On the Divine Images*. Trans. David Anderson. Crestwood, NY: St. Vladimir's Seminary Press, 1980.

Kelly, J. N. D. *Early Christian Creeds*. London and New York: Longman, 1991.

_____. *Early Christian Doctrines*. San Francisco: HarperCollins, 1978.

L'Huillier, Peter. *The Church of the Ancient Councils*. Crestwood, NY: St. Vladimir's Seminary Press, 1995.

Lossky, Vladimir. *The Mystical Theology of the Eastern Church*. London: James Clarke, 1957.

Margerie, Bertrand de. *The Christian Trinity in History*. Still River MA: St. Bede's Publications, 1982.

Meyendorff, John. *Christ in Eastern Thought*. Crestwood, NY: St. Vladimir's Seminary Press, 1975.

Moore, Peter C. *Man, Women and Priesthood*. London: SPCK, 1978.

Pelikan, Jaroslav. *The Christian Tradition: A History of the Development of Doctrine*. Vol. 1, *The Emergence of the Catholic Tradition (100-600)*. Vol. 2, *The Spirit of Eastern Christendom (600-1700)*. Chicago: University of Chicago Press, 1972, 1974.

Percival, H. R. *The Seven Ecumenical Councils of the Undivided Church*. Vol. 14 of the *Nicene and Post-Nicene Fathers, Second Series*. Peabody, MA: Hendrickson Publishers, Inc., 1994. [Originally published in 1900.]

Prestige, G. L. *Fathers and Heretics*. London: SPCK, 1948.

_____. *God in Patristic Thought*. London: William Heineman, 1936.

Relton, Herbert. M. *A Study in Christology*. London: SPCK, 1917.

Schaff, Philip, ed. *A Select Library of Nicene and Post-Nicene Fathers of the Christian Church*. 14 vols., Second Series. New York: Christian Literature Company, 1890-1900; reprint, Peabody, MA: Hendrickson Publishers, Inc., 1994.

Sellers, R. V. *The Council of Chalcedon*. London: SPCK, 1953.

_____. *Two Ancient Christologies: A Study in the Christological Thought of the Schools of Alexandria and Antioch*. London: SPCK, 1954.

Stead, G. C. *Divine Substance*. Oxford: Clarendon Press, 1977.

Stevenson, J. *A New Eusebius: Documents Illustrative of the History of the Church to A.D. 337*. London: SPCK, 1957.

_____. *Creeds, Councils and Controversies: Documents Illustrative of the History of the Church, A.D. 337-461*. London: SPCK, 1966.

Tanner, N. F. *Decrees of the Ecumenical Councils*. 2 vols. London and Washington, DC: Georgetown University Press, 1990.

Toon, Peter. *Our Triune God: A Biblical Portrayal of the Trinity*. Wheaton, IL: Victor Books, 1996.

Wainwright, A. W. *The Trinity in the New Testament*. London: SPCK, 1965.

INDEX